The Living Earth Handbook

Creating Sustainability from the Inside Out

Renee Wade

NATURAL COLLABORATION
NORTH SAN JUAN, CA

Natural Collaboration
PO Box 583
N San Juan, CA 95960
www.naturalcollaboration.com

The author offers the information in this book, and the reader accepts it, with the understanding that people act on any information contained herein at their own risk and with full knowledge that they should consult with medical professionals for any medical assistance they need. The author and publisher shall have neither liability, nor responsibility to any person or entity with respect to any loss, damage, or injury caused, or alleged to by caused, directly or indirectly, by the information provided in this book.

Cover Illustration © 2016 by Randi Griffis
Book Layout © 2016 BookDesignTemplates.com
Cover Design by Melissa Heiser

The Living Earth Handbook/ Renee Wade. -- 1st ed.
Print Edition ISBN 978-0-9979381-1-1
Kindle Edition ISBN 978-0-9979381-0-4

Library of Congress Control Number 2016913591

For Gaia,
mother, mentor, and friend.
You are the biggest love of my life.

And for Sun,
You are the electric light that makes the world go round.

Contents

Introduction

In botany, a *radicle* is the root that emerges from the seed. It's the part of the plant that first goes out exploring, later transforming into many roots. In time-lapse photography these roots resemble earthworms, looking very lively as they feel their way through the soil, pausing to sniff at this darker patch here, snacking from the buffet over there, or stopping to dance with the fungal mycelia a bit further on. The root is the part of the plant that digs deep into the soil, meets the neighbors, gathers needed food or water, offers sustenance to allies, and develops connections. The root gathers and sends both nutrients and information to the whole of the plant, anchoring it firmly in a world of active relationship and meaning.

My mother first called me *radical* when I was seventeen. I was actively engaged in exploring this place we call Earth and this thing we call Reality. Like any root, I wanted to dig deep and find nourishment from the world around me. I wanted to develop beneficial relationships with the people and things I encountered. I wanted to understand how the world works. I instinctively knew that in order to do so I had to question much and look below the surface of both people and things. I assumed that my mother – and most other people – would be interested in this information. Her frustrated tone, however, made it clear that *radical* was not meant as a complement. It was only later, when I discovered the word's connection to roots, that I realized how accurate her statement was, and redefined it for myself as an encouragement.

This book is for all of you who are also radicles, who spend your time digging deep and looking for root causes and synergistic solutions. This book is about my journey as a radicle. It is about what I have discovered and what I now know, both about myself and about the world around me. This is also a book about roots, because it is a book about connection and relationship.

A Root Called Agriculture

My personal journey has been centered around food and growing food for three decades now. Nature is the first love of my life, and it led me to reject an Ivy League education and attend instead a "radical" college in Washington State. I spent my first two years there immersing myself in natural history and environmental education programs. I loved my experiences in those two years, feeling as though I had found an oasis and refuge after years of loneliness growing up in urban Los Angeles. The forested campus gave me ample opportunity to become enveloped in the healing energies of the wild world, and I happily spent many hours watching the birds on Puget Sound and identifying the plants around me.

I knew, however, that this wild world was endangered. Over and over, in class after class, I learned about the threats to this natural world I so dearly loved. Over and over, in class after class, I learned that agriculture was perhaps the prime threat to this refuge of wildness - and that was a problem for me - because I eat. I eat food grown by agriculture. In the interval between my sophomore and junior year, I made the decision to change course, and leave behind the career in ecology or environmental education that had seemed so certain. I followed instead my desire to get to root causes, and so I enrolled in one of the few ecological agriculture programs then existing. I began my life as a food grower, ultimately becoming someone who practices ecology as a way of life.

The threats to the world around us are real, and my understanding of their complexity has grown with the years, yet the insight that agriculture plays a pivotal role in our current ecological dilemmas was and is correct. We live in a highly technical society where most people spend more time surrounded by machines than surrounded by plants or animals. Walls separate us from the elements of wind and rain or cold and heat, and yet agriculture is still what powers us. *Agriculture is still the root nourishing our civilization.* We do not eat electricity or petroleum, and the kind of agriculture we have built with petroleum is sickening us as well as the planet.

The distance between the vast majority of Americans and the agricultural systems that feed them is long, and we are paying for that distance with our health, our democracy, and our happiness. As a root of civilization, agriculture shapes our civilization, affecting every system it supports, from business and economy, to health and medical care, to energy and environment. When the food we eat comes from systems that kill the living soil, despoil and waste our water, and disrupt the health of the plants and animals that become our food, then a crucial link in our own health is broken. Food is created through the alchemical transformation, by plants and animals, of sunlight and minerals into nourishing molecules. Creating your own direct relationship to all the parts of this transformative system is the best way to create an agriculture that will sustain you in the challenging years ahead. This book can help you take steps to shorten the distance between you and the community of plants, animals, microbes, and soil that feeds you; steps that will strengthen your own roots, enriching every facet of your well-being.

Finding an Accurate Map

It was while I was exploring how to do agriculture in a way that works with nature, that I began to uncover a deeper aspect to our dilemma, or rather to realize that there was much more to it than how we do agriculture. In every human endeavor, there already exist technologies, ideas, and processes that are far more environmentally benign than current standard practices. As I passed through the 1980's and 1990's, I saw developments in every field from passive solar and natural building to the development of wind and solar electric technologies to alternative currencies such as the Ithaca dollar. Organic agriculture began to grow exponentially - and yet somehow the environmental news always seemed to be getting worse.

Why is it so hard to adopt different strategies? Why does it seem so easy for those different strategies to get watered down, co-opted, or to simply disappear? Passive solar and natural building strategies, for example, continue to be used only on the fringes. The demand for organic foods now often outstrips the supply, however, the standards behind the organic label are under attack every year as industrial-scale farms seek to earn profits without the same concern for environmental care with which the organic movement began.

How can we make real changes and get them to stick? The answer is surprisingly simple. Our choices, actions, and behaviors are driven by the stories that we believe and the ideas we hear repeated over and over again. We each hold a very powerful tool, one that most people have not yet recognized with the clarity it deserves, even though we all use it every day. That tool is *story*.

Stories are roots. They are the below ground part of us, the part that feeds and nourishes and connects us to every part of our world. Stories are the filter and organizer for our perceptions, and how we filter and organize our perceptions determines whether our experiences become food and sustenance for our journeys or undigested molecules that clog our systems. Our stories influence us at the level of our DNA. The emerging science of epigenetics has discovered that, while our DNA carries the code for our bodies, those genes can be switched on or switched off by our environment. Stories are a critical part of our internal and external environment, and they can play a big role in how our DNA operates. Stories can create an effective and strong root system, supporting us in our life journeys; or stories can create a weak and ineffective root system, one that cannot support our growth and evolution.

The story that we are most commonly told about ourselves and about the world we live in, the shared world-view that drives our decisions and actions, is killing us because it is not true. We are working from a warped and distorted map, one that pictures the Earth as a solid, round ball floating in empty space, while failing to see in our planet the round, living cell that intelligently connects us all to a living, plasma-filled universe. The map we have been using cannot take us to health or prosperity or sustainability because it does not accurately represent the world we live in or the relationships that create that world.

I have seen the impacts of my stories play out in my own organic farming and gardening evolution. In its nascent stage – and this stage is still the most common form - organic agriculture is a softer form of conventional agriculture. We spray aphids with biodegradable soaps, rather than the harsher, longer-lasting, and more toxic chemical options. We till our soil and then add compost and soft rock phosphate, not a bag of 16-16-16. We claim to "feed the soil, not the plant," and while organic agriculture often does take better care of soil than conventional agriculture, organic practitioners also spend a lot of time foliar feeding plants with organic forms of fertilizer to enhance yields and overcome the problems created by unbalanced soils low in organic matter. The people practicing this nascent form of organics tell a very similar story to the story told by conventional agriculturists. They often use battle language, speaking of "pests" and "threats" and "eradication," as they fight the good fight to grow our food.

Like many others, I started from this place. I would see insects eating the plants in my gardens, and I would feel threatened and reach for a spray bottle of "organic" poison. I would see a plant that was not thriving, and I would feel disheartened and try to feed it, also often from a bottle. Until one balmy, early summer day in Sacramento, when I walked into my garden and noticed that I felt stressed and worried and that I was not having fun. I decided then that I was done with the war to grow food. I was done with the battle mentality. I would find a way to truly work with nature. Finding that way has meant, more than anything, *changing the framework that I use to understand the world and my relationship to it.* I have found and learned to live in a different story.

Modern science is on the cusp of a completely new understanding of physical reality, a shift even bigger than the one we made when we discovered that the earth was round, not flat. My own explorations of the discoveries of microbiology, neurobiology, quantum physics, epigenetics, and plasma physics have helped me to formulate a clearer understanding of both my inner experience and the outer world. The universe is a much richer and more magnificent place than standard texts let on. There is a new story emerging - a young radicle - and it offers all of us a path to deep well-being and a healthy, balanced relationship with this wondrous, living earth. This book will get you started on that path and connect you to that young root.

Yes! It's Alive!

I remember clearly my conviction when I was a young child that the world was fully alive in all its parts, immensely creative, and magical to the core. I was thrilled to be able to be a part of such magnificence, and I eagerly looked forward to becoming an adult because I was also convinced that adults were fully empowered, creative people.

While I am again convinced of the first part of that equation – that the world is a fully alive, creative, and magical place - I have learned that being an adult is not so straightforward as I had thought. I didn't understand the modern process of developing from child to adult. I didn't understand the extent to which so many children and teens are guided, pushed, and dragged into becoming less-than-empowered and not-too-creative adult versions of themselves.

Fortunately, the fully alive, immensely creative, and magical to the core part of each of us is impossible to destroy or dismantle. It can be buried, and it may take a bit of digging to find, but it is always there. This book is designed to help you find that part of yourself. The simple practices contained at the end of each chapter will help you to dust yourself off and give the creative and magical part of you some exercise. You will discover the new science of the heart and learn about the heart's connection to the nervous system. This is a science that opened unexpected doors for me, and these discoveries are a central part of this book and of the practices at the end of each chapter. These are discoveries which will help you to root deeply and to nourish yourself so fully that it becomes impossible to live apart from your central, creative core.

This central and creative heart-core is important because it is an integral part of your connection to the living Earth. When this part of you is actively nourished, you will find that you cease to be separate from nature. Your days as a "tourist," one who happens to live on a beautiful planet, will be over. You will rediscover your ability to be indigenous, no matter what your genetic background. You will know in both heart and mind that you are an important member of this planetary organism.

A deep understanding that this world we live in is indeed a living organism, not a machine, is a critical part of our new story root. Many of our ancestors knew this truth, and many children still know this truth – that we are living beings on a living planet in a living universe. I suspect that you, who are attracted to read this book, also know this truth, but find it difficult to articulate it in public. I offer to you in these pages a more comprehensive framework for understanding and living in this simple truth.

Many scientists are now warning us that we have entered the era of the Earth's sixth Great Extinction. A web is unraveling – just as we are beginning to understand it. The wonderful thing about a living planet and a living universe is that there is a tremendous capacity for repair, regeneration, and reorganization. We are now fairly certain that the demise of the dinosaurs, the era of the fifth Great Extinction, was caused by a comet striking the Earth in the Gulf of Mexico, near the Yucatan. In a dead universe, on a round ball of a planet, such an accident could easily have led only to chaos and a final ending. Instead, it led to a great flowering – literally. The demise of the dinosaurs led to the era when flowering plants first blossomed across Earth, and the mammal population exploded. Perhaps that comet was not some icy, dead rock, but more like a sperm. It was likely a home to microbes of some kind, and those microbes would have been quickly dispersed to the far reaches of the globe on the massive clouds of water vapor sent up by the impact. What did those microbes teach the indigenous microbes of Earth? What new information did they share, and did it help to create that massive flowering which we still enjoy today?

Do you see how a change in story can open up new possibilities and new adventures?

It seems likely to be too late to avoid this sixth era of extinctions, but I have tremendous hope for Earth's future and for humanity's future because I know that we are one living organism. As we change our story-root and learn to work together, we will accomplish what, from today's perspective, would seem to be miracles.

The Gift of Leverage

A lever is an ancient tool that gives more power or energy to your effort. With a lever, you can lift something that is too heavy for you to lift directly. A lever is a magnifier and multiplier, making it possible to do things that otherwise seem to be impossible. I knew the theory of a fulcrum and lever, and thought I understood it, but until the day I was trying to move a heavy rock for a garden wall, I didn't really get it. The boyfriend who would one day be my husband watched me heave and push on that rock for several minutes before he quietly went and got a small rock and a long, thick metal rod – a rock bar.

"Try these," he said, as he offered me these simple tools.

I contemplated his offerings, then invited him to help me place them properly to direct the rock in the desired direction. Within a minute the rock was in place. I knew the physical principles that we had just applied, but it still felt like magic. All that work accomplished with so little effort.

The many stories in this book create one story, and that one story is a lever. It is a story of creative awareness, intelligent interconnection, and deep collaboration creating a living planet in a living universe. This bigger story is the tool we need if we are to rapidly shift our experience from struggle to embrace, from isolation to connection, from scarcity to abundance. This is a story that can carry us from fragmentation to wholeness as it roots us firmly in the web of relationships that create this living world. It is a story that can nurture each of us individually while also guiding us into our next evolutionary step, one of living in conscious and creative collaboration with Earth.

One

Curious Awareness is Your Magic Key

I suffered from chronic lower back pain for three decades, from my mid-teens to my mid-forties. It was never debilitating, but it was nagging and sometimes draining. I have always been an active person, so this was not about too much time at a desk. I ran cross-country and studied dance in high school and became an avid hiker and gardener after that, so staying strong and being in good health was always high on my agenda. I tried yoga, stretching, chiropractic, and a variety of other massage and body-work modalities to fix the back pain, but relief never lasted for more than a few hours.

Then I got lucky. I heard about a 4-week series of classes, called So-matics, being offered at our rural community center. The description sounded intriguing, and the price and timing were right, so I signed up. The class was taught by a sparkling-eyed, white-haired, 60-year-old woman named Yahdi. Her enthusiasm for bodies and for life was infectious.

Somatics is about becoming aware of your body and its movement with a level of detail that I had never before experienced. We spent most of the class lying on the floor, slowly repeating motions, many of which I would not have thought to try on my own. For example, in one of the lessons, I lay on my stomach with my left hand facing palm down and under my head which was turned to lie facing left. I then slowly lifted the left elbow and the right leg simultaneously and then returned them to the ground, while paying exquisite attention to how the muscles in my shoulders, back, and other body parts moved and worked. Yahdi's gentle voice guided us through these motions while directing our attention to the many details involved in moving.

At the end of the four classes, I noticed that my back was feeling much better, so I signed up for the next level, another 4-week session. These were somewhat more complex motions, but the basic pattern of movement coupled with attention never changed. By the end of the second series, my back was cured. It happened so gradually over those 8 weeks that I didn't notice when it stopped aching; I just noticed one day that my back didn't hurt – at all. Wow! There were a few backslides in the first year after the class, but by repeating the most basic of the exercises on my own with the same deep attention to my body, the pain would be gone again the following day. Seven years later, I don't know when my lower back last ached. It's been years.

Attention and awareness healed what had been a chronic and intractable problem. I did not need surgery, or a lifetime of weekly visits to a medical professional, or steroids or other chemicals pumped into my system. I simply needed a framework for becoming aware of my body. Yahdi never directed me to change anything, she only asked me to notice. The changes that occurred were well outside the realm of my rational mind. They occurred in a state with no judgement, only pure awareness and curiosity.

Curious awareness is our most powerful tool. With it, we can change anything.

The Creative Nature of Observation

Can awareness and observation impact the reality outside our bodies? Are they truly effective at changing the inside of our bodies? The experiments of quantum physics have given us many scientific observations

THE LIVING EARTH HANDBOOK

demonstrating a deep connection between matter and consciousness, between observation and our seemingly solid reality. In laboratories around the world, the double-slit experiment has demonstrated for over one hundred years now, that the building blocks of the material world exist only as energy *unless they are being carefully observed.* In this experiment a beam of light or a flow of electrons is passed through a chamber containing a partition with two narrow rectangles cut into it – hence the term "double slit experiment." After the light or electrons pass through these two rectangular openings, they hit a screen, leaving an impression of their passing.

This experiment was originally used in 1802 to demonstrate that light was not composed of solid particles, but was more akin to a fluid, moving like the ripples on a pond or the swells of the deep ocean. As a beam of light was sent into the chamber, it was split into two by the two rectangles. The two waves, or ripples, of light left a pattern of regular and repeating stripes on the back screen as they alternately amplified or cancelled each other out.

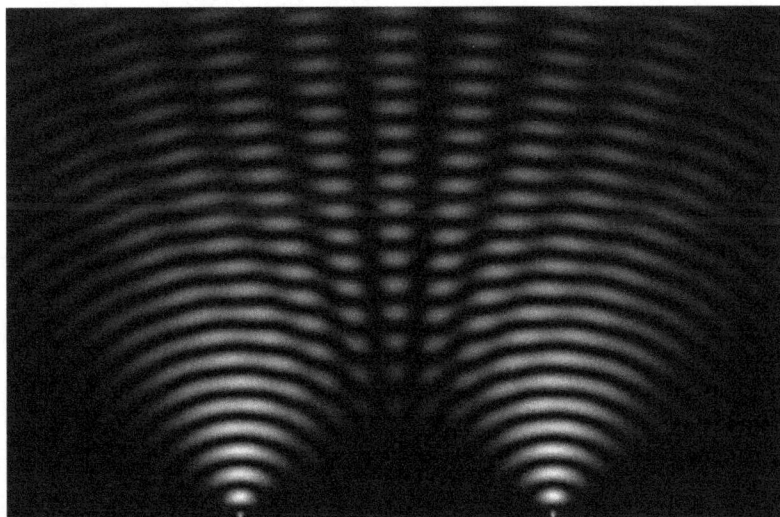

Figure 1: Light waves in the double slit experiment. Notice the vertical black stripes that appear as some of the waves cancel each other. From Wikimedia Commons.

By the end of the nineteenth century electrons were known to be solid particles, so their passage through the two slits was expected to result in two dense blobs on the final screen. Instead, the electron beam produced the repeating, striped pattern of a non-solid wave. The electrons were behaving as though they were pure energy with no mass at all.

This got even more crazy and interesting when sensors were put into the partition with the double slits to measure which of the two openings the electron particles were passing through. When these sensors were activated, the electrons behaved like particles, leaving the two blob pattern on the back screen. This experiment continues to be replicated in labs around the world, each time demonstrating that matter is affected by consciousness, by attention, by awareness. Energy waves do crystallize into things when measured.

These experiments remind me of the old Zen koan: if a tree falls in a forest and no one is there to hear it, did it make a noise? Perception is a key facet to being alive. Every organism that is alive, from the smallest bacteria to the largest whale to planet Earth, perceives its environment in some way. Life is a multifaceted community of many perceptive organisms, including us as humans. A tree can't be in a forest without being witnessed by the other organisms of the forest. However, if all perception were to cease, would the tree still exist as a solid form? My guess is no. This is the deeper lesson of quantum physics; without perceptual awareness, without consciousness, none of what we call solid and real could exist in a solid form. *Consciousness is the soil that grows our physical reality.*

Not all physicists are willing to draw this conclusion from the double-slit experiment, primarily because this conclusion violates an assumption made in the early days of science, namely that matter produces consciousness, not the other way around. Science has never proven that matter preceded consciousness. It is an assumption, dating from the beginnings of science. Early scientists needed matter to be separate from consciousness in order to avoid upsetting the Catholic Church and drawing the attention of the Inquisition. Because the Church taught that God had created nature but was not in nature (as many Christians still believe), studying nature (solid matter) was possible and safe only so long as it was kept separate from God – and consciousness and intelligence.

Our inability to create a sustainable or regenerative society and culture is rooted in both these scientific and Christian stories of separation because these stories leave us with no sense of intelligent and creative connection to all that surrounds us. So long as consciousness and intelligence are outside nature, nature can only be random, meaningless, and machine-like. We are prevented from perceiving that we are embedded in a fabric, or a soil, rich in relationship and entanglement continually creating this living universe in each moment. Physicist Amit Goswami of the University of Oregon has become one of an increasing number of scientists willing to step aside from this basic assumption that matter precedes consciousness. In his book, *The Self-Aware Universe: How Consciousness Creates the Material World*, he says,

> *If initial conditions do not forever determine an object's motion, if instead every time we observe, there is a new beginning, then the world is creative at the base level.... Every event of measurement [observation] is potentially creative and may open new possibilities.*

Quantum physics demonstrates that atomic "particles" flow easily between solid and energy states. An interaction with awareness is what causes them to shift to solid form and to a determined position in time and space. This shows me that interactions and relationships are fundamental not just to living things but to all things. The interactions that consciousness and awareness provide are a fundamental property of the universe, they are the living soil from which the living universe grows.

I also find the double-slit experiment interesting because the scientists performing it do not need to *intend* for matter to manifest out of energy; they do not need to use willpower to create electrons as particles. They use only that pure form of curious awareness which I discovered in my Somatics classes; they take measurements of what is happening, and that act of measuring somehow changes energy into matter. We do not need to understand how this happens, but it is helpful to know that it does happen. Curious awareness is the power of measuring and the power of growing reality.

Does Consciousness Organize Life?

Biologist Rupert Sheldrake is another example of a scientist who is willing to question science's basic assumptions, including the assumption that consciousness comes from matter. He has conducted many explorations into consciousness, not at the quantum scale, but at the scale of our everyday lives. His curiosity was first piqued as he conducted research into developmental biology, the study of how living organisms grow and develop. His research showed him that the protein building know-how of our genes was not enough to explain how those proteins became organized into functioning organs and skeletal structures. This is a problem which has confronted many developmental biologists since the 1920's.

The generally accepted concept in biology at this time is that "fields" supply the wholistic and organizational intelligence needed to put the right protein and the right cell in the right place to create, say, a heart or a spleen. Think of a magnetic field, that invisible force that extends outside the body of a magnet, shifting the position of iron filings, for example, or spinning the needle on a compass. Many biologists believe that chemicals create the energetic fields that guide the development of our bodies, but Sheldrake has a different idea. His theory of morphic fields postulates the existence of fields that originate from consciousness; these fields organize physical processes but are not created by physical processes. Morphic fields are "non-local," meaning they exist outside the physical confines of space and time. In the same way that a magnet organizes random iron filings into a pattern, these morphic fields are information-dense, non-material consciousness organizing and guiding the growth and development of individual organisms in repeating and recognizable patterns.

In Sheldrake's theory, each species has its own morphic field, its own collection of templates and patterns to which all individuals of that species have access. Morphic fields grow and change, thus allowing species to evolve; the experience of each individual flows into the field, creating new templates and patterns over time. This is how poodles could evolve from wolves. As a subset of wolves morphed into dogs, the morphic field of wolves would have first stretched and expanded, and then divided, perhaps much the way our cells divide in order to reproduce. Poodles, as a subset of dogs, would be part of the dog morphic field, with a special section devoted to their unique patterns of structure and behavior.

To imagine the human morphic field, imagine a virtual library containing all the learning and experience of every person who has ever held human form. All the languages spoken, all the sports and games ever invented, all the music or drawings ever made would be housed here in some way. Everyone has the ability both to add to this library and to access the information it contains. The more current the information, meaning the more living people who are actively using it, the easier it is to access that information, much like an internet search engine showing the most active websites at the top of a list.

Sheldrake has devised many experiments to test for the possible existence of this field. He has found, for example, that crossword puzzles, the ones published in newspapers, are easier to solve at the end of a day than they are in the morning. When a puzzle is first published, a relatively small number of people have solved it. As the day wears on, more and more people will have solved its riddles. Each time this happens, that learning is stored in the human morphic field. Because we are each connected to that field, those who are working on crossword puzzles in the evening will be unknowingly helped by those who solved it earlier in the day; their brains will jump more quickly to the right answer because that answer is active in the field.

Sheldrake has uncovered much evidence that gives credence to the existence of morphic fields, and more information about his work is in the Resources section at the end of this book. Morphic fields show us a non-physical template through which consciousness becomes capable of creating a consistent and organized physical reality that also evolves. That template is shaped through the awareness and attention each individual gives to their life experience. It is not a final blueprint, but an active field of patterns and unfolding possibilities that changes as we change. I have come to think of consciousness as soil-like, and I see morphic fields as a root system in that soil, one that consciousness uses to nourish and grow a physical world.

The Cost of Awareness

Our awareness and attention are energies capable of growing fields and creating physical effects. Using that awareness requires energy. When my husband broke his leg at the age of 58, we found that traditional physical therapy could only take him so far towards a complete recovery. Fortunately, by then, we had discovered another body awareness practice, Feldenkrais. This is a system that holds many similarities to the Somatics classes I had taken, but uses completely different exercises to bring awareness to the body.

My husband had thrown away his cane, but still walked with a heavy limp when he began taking weekly Feldenkrais classes. After just one class, his improvement was noticeable. After ten weeks, he was back to climbing trees and doing his own gardening.

I decided to join him at the classes to see what benefits I would derive. I had no particular agenda, but immediately started noticing a feeling of being taller and more balanced. My neck began to glide more easily from side-to-side, even though I had not thought it to be stiff when I began the classes. My overall sense of well-being increased – except for right after class.

I came out of my first three classes feeling famished. Then I noticed that in the first few hours after class little things would strongly annoy me. The cat jumping on the kitchen counter or the phone in an unusual place were causes for mini-tantrums. My body was requiring huge amounts of energy to process the learning embedded in each class, and I wasn't giving it the extra it needed to do that smoothly and easily.

I began a practice of eating high-protein foods before the class – a bowl of bone-broth rich soup with high-quality beef or chicken, for example. I paid extra attention to my breathing during and after class to be sure I was keeping my body well-oxygenated. I planned for filling and nutrient-dense dinners after class, and made sure my body was well-hydrated. I kept that evening's calendar mostly free, so that I could get to sleep early and give my brain extra time to process. All of this extra self-care allowed the rest of my after class experiences to be easier and tension-free. It also made it possible for me to integrate a maximum amount of improvement in my function from each class.

The experience of reading this book may cause a similar experience for you as I bring your attention to places and things that may be new or may be upside-down to what seems normal and accepted. Awareness may seem like an effortless thing compared to running or jumping, but brains and nervous systems operate at a huge cost in energy and nutrition. Taking good care of yourself is the first step to making the deep-rooted, foundational shifts that allow for better flows of energy in your body and mind, making it possible to integrate new information and new patterns of thinking. I invite you to pause here and notice if your body needs any care right now. A deep breath? A drink of water? A stretch?

Playtime! Connect to Your Senses

Young children are the most skilled of all learners. The amount of growth they experience, the number of new skills they develop, and the quantity of new information they integrate is astounding. I am repeatedly impressed by the capacities of people under the age of six.

One of the reasons for this impressive learning capacity is that young children are also wonderfully adept at play. They have not yet been taught to take learning seriously, and so they do what comes naturally. They play at crawling, then they play at standing, and then they play at stepping out and walking. They play with the sound of their voices, learning to repeat those sounds that get happy reactions from Mom or Dad. Everything they do is play.

The easiest way for any of us to learn anything is through play. Unfortunately, most of us have forgotten how to use this capacity, especially when we have a strong desire to learn something, because the attitude of seriousness is generally much preferred in schools.

At the end of each chapter, you will find a playtime exercise. These are mostly simple practices that you can add to your everyday life. Please approach them as play. Adapt them as you need, so that they can be fun and enjoyable. If you find yourself feeling tense or anxious as you do them, stop and take a breath. There is no test coming. Accept your starting point. Let yourself fall down repeatedly, as babies do when learning to walk. As you lay on the ground, figuratively speaking, congratulate yourself for trying, cheer yourself on, and then get up and take a nap if need be, but do return to let yourself play again. This is how new skills are built.

Our first playtime exercise is an exploration of awareness. We have many senses, but we often forget to use them. Connecting with your senses is one of the most healing things you can do for yourself, and it is free. Noticing your environment will automatically slow your heart-rate and your breathing. It will lead to a greater sense of ease and of calm. It will center you in the most powerful of all moments: Now.

Begin by finding a comfortable place to sit, preferably outside. It can be a balcony or backyard, a park or an ocean beach. Choosing someplace that feels safe is important. Ideally, it is also a place with plants, birds, insects, and animals.

Next, take some time to settle yourself comfortably in a sitting position. It helps to be comfortable and relaxed, but it also helps tremendously if your spine is straight, so take some time if you need to arrange chairs, pillows, or other props.

Now, take a breath. Then do it again, noticing how that breath feels. Does it move your shoulders, your belly, or both? There is no right or wrong here. Awareness of what is; that is all you are after.

Now, close your eyes and listen. What is the furthest away sound that you can hear? What is the closest sound that you hear? Breathe. How many sounds do you hear? There is no need to put a name to anything you hear. Experiencing what you notice is all that is necessary.

Move next to your sense of smell, keeping your eyes closed if that is comfortable. What do you smell? Perhaps you can identify it, or maybe describe it, but do experience it. The main idea is to simply notice whatever your nose is noticing. Do you smell more than one smell? Breathe.

What about your sense of taste? What are your taste buds noticing? Again, experiencing it is enough. Breathe again.

Next, move on to your sense of touch. What sensations are coming from your skin? Do you feel a breeze on your face? Do you feel your clothes on your body? Are you warm or cold? What does that fly crawling on your arm actually feel like? What else is your skin noticing? Breathe.

Open your eyes now, and let them relax. Looking straight in front of you, notice what is on the edges of your vision. No need to bring those edges into focus by looking directly at them. It is more important here to let your eyes remain relaxed, perhaps noticing the swaying movement of a branch or the blur of a bird flying past on the periphery of your sight. Breathe.

Now that you have connected with all five senses, take a moment to stretch. Notice if you feel any different. Has your mood changed? Does your body feel any different than it did before you started? Again, there is no right or wrong answer here. The only goal is to use your awareness and notice what is.

This is an exercise that you can do as often as you like. You can spend three minutes doing it, or twenty. When you are first playing with it, I suggest being outside in a natural setting as that is the best place to be for maximum relaxation benefits, but eventually you may want to play with this exercise while standing in line at the grocery store or while eating dinner. The simple act of bringing your awareness fully to the place where you are can change everything. Try it.

As extra assistance, audio versions of each of the playtime exercises in this book are available through my website. Please visit: https://NaturalCollaboration.com

Two

Our Story Power is Creative

Storytelling is possibly the oldest of the arts. It helps to form the fabric of every culture, and creates the connective tissue of every family. I have the good fortune to be married to a master storyteller, someone who can gather and hold the attention of any audience (at least any that I have seen) as he weaves a tale that engages all the senses and takes listeners on a vivid journey. I took a photo once, many years ago, of a circle of our friends as they listened to my husband weave an impromptu story. In it our friends sit mesmerized, with every one of their mouths hanging open. Over time, witnessing many such scenes, I have come to appreciate the very real power of stories.

When my husband tells a story, he can completely change the mood of his audience. To be honest, this used to cause me great concern. His collection of stories in those early years was skewed in a direction that often felt dark and disempowering from my perspective. I didn't like what he could do to the "vibe." As he has become more aware of the influence his stories have, he has also become more committed to telling stories that help people to feel happier and more powerful, and I now love having people come up to me, sometimes years after hearing one of my husband's performances, to tell me how much that story has stuck with them, making them smile and feel good.

The words of a story create a framework, a format, which colors our perspective and influences our interpretations of the events and experiences that make up our lives. The stories we tell and believe are critical because we act and behave in alliance with our stories. For example, are you terrified of bacteria and microbes, knowing that these enemies to your health are hanging out on the cutting board in your kitchen and hitchhiking on the hands of your friends and enemies alike? Or are you in love with bacteria and microbes? Are these intelligent ancestors and benefactors the means to great health as they teach your immune system about its environment and assist you in every possible way?

If you believe the first story, you will undoubtedly rely on antibacterial soaps and keep your home spotless. It is also likely that you or your children suffer from several colds every year as well as allergies and possibly asthma. If you believe the second story, you probably eat humus-rich dirt along with your carrots, let your dog lick your face, and rarely suffer from colds, flu, or allergies. Stories do influence our daily choices and actions, creating consequences that cascade throughout our lives.

From Placebos to Firewalking

Medical science has recognized the strong power of stories for centuries and has many documented cases of patients getting better when given a placebo – a sugar pill or other benign substance that has been dressed up by a story and is masquerading as something more potent. Developments in neuroimaging now allow scientists to track the effects of an injection, be it a real drug or a placebo containing only a saline solution. They have found that a saline solution that is presented to the patient as a potent drug in the fight against Parkinson's is just as capable of increasing dopamine production in their brain as is the actual drug. A placebo creates real effects, not just imagined ones. The Placebo Effect is so prevalent and powerful that drug manufacturers must demonstrate in their drug trials that their medicine is more effective than a "mere" placebo.

Dr. Bruce Moseley is a surgeon who performed a placebo-controlled arthroscopic knee surgery trial on a group of ten patients in 1994. Both the group receiving real surgery and the group that received fake surgery recovered the function of their knees – and those in the placebo surgery group retained those improvements even after they learned which group they had been in. According to a 2013 article in the Wall Street Journal, a similar placebo-controlled surgery study was performed in Finland with similar results. When people believe in the power of either a substance or an event to do good in their bodies, the body is able to heal itself.

Another way to understand the powerful effects that our stories and beliefs have on our experience is through the analogy of computers. Our brains are often compared to our high-tech, silicon-based computers, and in many ways, they do seem to resemble carbon-based supercomputers evolved through eons of research and development. (As computers learn to learn, we may find the line between animate and inanimate is subtler than we thought, and that electricity crosses that line.) Computers are amazing tools, but it's the software that makes a computer useful. I am typing this on a well-designed, finely-tuned machine, but without the word processing software that takes in this typing and allows it to be formatted to a page, the computer would be worthless to me. Typing this in the wrong software, say a spreadsheet system, would make this writing experience an exercise in sheer frustration as I tried to use the wrong tool to get me to my desired result.

In the human body-mind system, stories are our software. Stories are the programs that we run on the "hard drive" of our body-minds, and there is no community that understands this better than those who firewalk. I took a firewalking workshop on a cold fall evening when I was 27-years-old. The workshop was held on a spacious estate in Marin County, California, and consisted mostly of stories. Our workshop leader, a young, dark-haired, wiry man named Jon Cotton, spent hours telling us vivid stories about the power of the human mind to influence our bodies and abilities. Most of his stories were about fire.

I remember one story in particular that he related to us, told to him by a woman whom he had met while teaching an earlier firewalking workshop. This woman, I will call her Barbara, had been present on two different camping adventures where a toddler had tripped and fallen into a hot campfire. The first time this happened, the mother had quickly snatched the child from the fire and immediately begun wailing, "My child is burned! My child is burned!" The burns that this child sustained were quite severe and required hospitalization.

The second time Barbara witnessed a toddler fall into a hot campfire, the mother again quickly snatched her child from the fire, but this mother immediately began to rock her child, saying to it, "You're fine. You're fine." This second toddler sustained no burns whatsoever. From Barbara's perspective, there was little difference in the intensity of the fire or the time the child spent in the fire. It was the mothers' responses and communications to the children that were clearly different. The story software these mothers offered to their young and easily impressionable children – "you're burned" or "you're fine" – determined the outcome of the experience.

As the firewalking workshop progressed, Jon interspersed these kinds of powerful stories with forays outside to build and tend to our own bonfire. We lit at least a full cord of oak wood on fire that evening, then drummed and danced in rhythmic, swaying motions around it. Returning inside we were treated to more stories, stories designed to connect us to our inner wisdom as well as to our ability to walk on fire. We did a short meditation, then went back out to check on the fire with more drumming and dancing. The third time we ventured out, it was time to rake out the hot coals into a twelve-foot-long and 6 to 8-inch-deep pathway and then dance and drum our way across it. As I assisted with the raking, my upper body quickly broke into a sweat due to the intense heat.

The first rule of firewalking is to listen to your own inner guidance. Your body-mind knows if you are ready to go, but you have to be able to cut through any mental chatter – both the fear and the bravado – to discern that for yourself. The dancing and drumming help to quiet that chatter and let the inner wisdom through to conscious awareness. Jon's advice as we danced up to the super-hot pathway for our first pass: if you feel that "yes," don't hesitate and don't linger, walk confidently and quickly across.

I danced up to the coals and felt a clear "yes, go!" My Southern California feet were so cold by then that I wouldn't have known if they were being burned as I crossed the fire in five steps. Arriving on the other side, I felt my feet with my hands to be certain of their soundness, and then a wave of pure exhilaration swept through me. I crossed the coals more times than I counted that night, slowing way down and dancing my way across on my final round. My feet were fine, as were the feet of all those who walked that night, a whopping ninety percent of the participants from what I witnessed. No one had second degree burns. One woman reported a red spot of first degree burn, but she was clearly excited and empowered by her experience.

Firewalkers understand how to work with the hard drive of the human body-mind. The stories I listened to that night were software. To fully download those stories onto my hard drive required a different state of mind. I could receive the first part of the download while sitting and listening in the everyday consciousness of the beta brainwaves of my rational mind, but to fully integrate the download required slipping into alpha or theta states. The meditations and dancing and drumming created those deeper states and completed the installation.

Could I walk on fire today? This is a download that I haven't used since that night several decades ago. I know it's still stored on my hard drive, but I would want some help in finding it and refreshing it. Software, including story software, requires some upkeep in order to function properly. Just as your computer and mobile devices are constantly receiving updates, so too do our stories need regular updating to work efficiently.

Stories and beliefs have real effects in our bodies. They can help us to walk on super-hot coals and to heal our bodies of diseases. They also influence the choices and decisions we make and the ways in which we behave. Like all software, we have to choose the right program for the job. Most of what we see unfolding around us in the human world is the result of the software we run in our body-mind systems. The majority of stories that make up that software are designed to assist in warfare and domination. Those stories are a blueprint for the Apocalypse, but they cannot help us to create sustainability and joy.

Uncovering the Roots of Our Current Crisis

Modern society is a complex of interlocking financial, political, legal, educational, agricultural, and media systems. Most people I meet seem to agree that this "System" is in trouble, and there are many theories about what is wrong with it and what we need to do to change or morph it into something less harmful and more beneficial. Thousands, even hundreds of thousands, of non-profits and nongovernmental organizations around the globe are working on this every day. It seems clear that this System, or aspects of it, are the cause of our problems, and most people focus on changing the System in some way in order to create a better world, socially as well as environmentally.

Yet, what if this System, which I somewhat fondly like to call the Behemoth, is not the problem? What if the Behemoth is **not the cause, but merely a symptom of a deeper issue?** What if that deeper issue is our belief in a set of stories which do not give us accurate guidance in understanding the world around us? What if a change of story is the lever we need to use, or the radicle we need to water?

For people who suffer from allergies or arthritis, medical science can offer relief from symptoms, but it is not as good at offering a true cure. Antihistamines, decongestants, aspirin, or ibuprofen can help to mitigate the symptoms of these diseases, but they do not offer healing. What they offer is temporary relief. Prozac and Zoloft relieve the symptoms of depression, but they are not a cure. Wouldn't it be nice to have a real healing and to find an actual cure? Wouldn't it be wonderful to be done with the Zoloft and the Prozac, because our systems are in balance and don't need that daily dose of chemistry with all its possible side effects in order to function well? Wouldn't it be sweet to have systems in place all around us that made economic equality, social justice, and environmental well-being our natural trajectory?

The interlocking systems of the Behemoth all share a commonality. They are built from the same core beliefs, from the same stories. The ideas that led incrementally to the unfolding evolution of our economic system are the same ideas that structure government and medicine, education and energy development, and most of our agriculture. We hear the same stories repeated over and over, and we become certain that they must be true. Everyone knows that life is about the survival of the fittest, and that nature is "bloody in tooth and claw." We live in a "dog-eat-dog world, a machine-like universe that has no intrinsic purpose or meaning." These are the concepts that color our relationship with Earth.

We are told equally inaccurate stories about human beings: We are "fallen," and have been "evicted" from Eden, or we are "random bits of consciousness in an accidental world." "All humans are inherently selfish and greedy." "We are different than nature." "We are separate from all that surrounds us." These are the stories that color our relationships with each other and, more importantly, with ourselves.

Every system we depend on for survival is built upon these stories.

Think about it.

Will these ideas ever make you feel happy and safe?

Is it any wonder that we have the Behemoth?

These stories keep us, individually and collectively, locked into choices and actions that are harming us because they misrepresent and misguide us in our relationships with ourselves and with nature. If we wish to create real change, we need to learn – and believe – a very different story, a story of collaboration, belonging, and purpose. There are cultures on Earth who tell this different story, but their stories have seemed to fall on deaf ears. These alternate stories have not spoken compellingly to our rational minds. That is now changing. Scientists in many different fields, from microbiology and neurobiology to plasma and quantum physics, are finding the rational underpinnings of this different story, and are laying the ground for a radically new world-view.

The Guiding Light of Science

Before I explore the science now emerging that demonstrates how different the world is than what we have mostly been taught, I want to say a few things about science. Science is one of our greatest undertakings. To discover and understand the workings of the universe, including ourselves, in a methodical and organized fashion is a huge endeavor. There is much about science that I admire. I like its love of rationality and its determination to use objective experimentation – controlled experience – to find answers and solve the riddles posed by our existence. I like how science can and often does add insight to everyday life. I like many of the tools that we now have as a result of science, including the computer that is typing this book and the electrical system that provides power to that computer. Science is the reason we have washing machines and on-demand hot water, my two most favorite inventions to date.

Science is also a very human endeavor. It is being created and directed by real people with all the hang-ups of real people. Science is not perfect, and many scientists are quick to admit this. Scientists have the same concerns about money, status, and reputation as everyone else. They are part of an elite group, with special training. They have our attention. The set of words "scientific studies show..." are a powerful formula that gives authority and credence to whatever follows.

This used to be the situation for the Catholic church. It was the elite group with special training. It had the attention of all of Europe. What the pope, cardinal, bishop, or priest said was questioned only at great risk. Corruption ensued, as it always does when large sums of money and no outside oversight exist. Science is currently in similar trouble.

Scientists are real people, and the science they produce can be bought off and skewed to produce desired results – as opposed to hard facts and real truths. The mainstream media, for example, regularly reports that vaccines and genetically-modified foods are good for us, citing scientific studies as the basis for these statements. The odd thing is that the studies proving the value of vaccines and GMO foods are funded by the corporations that produce these products. The studies that are independently funded tend to reveal just the opposite, that these products hold grave dangers for us. The difference is all about design. Studies can be designed in ways that camouflage problems with vaccines or genetically-modified foods. Conclusions can be drawn that are not actually supported by the study data.

For example, in a study of vaccines, **both** the control group and the test subjects could receive a shot containing mercury, formaldehyde, and the other potentially toxic substances contained in the vaccine, with only the test subjects also receiving the bit of antigen that can confer resistance to a virus. Do you think this type of study would reveal problems related to the mercury and other substances in the vaccine? There is no true control group in such a study, yet this design has been used to prove that vaccines are safe for our children.

In many ways science has become our newest religion, complete with its own dogmas. Geneticists are particularly open about this, labeling their fondest theories as the "Central Dogma," but most branches of science have a road they have chosen, and they are loath to give up that road. In Cosmology, the Big Bang theory has become a dogma, with each new image from space being examined only through the lens of this story. No matter how difficult it becomes to fit the data we are gathering into this favored theory, no other theories are being entertained by serious astrophysicists, because to do so would ruin their careers. Interestingly, the Big Bang theory was originated by Georges Lemaitre who was both a trained astrophysicist and a Roman Catholic priest.

Even at its purest, science is a tricky undertaking, and I have learned to look carefully and ask questions before using it as a guide. I became a vegetarian at age 14 after reading *Diet for a Small Planet* by Frances Moore Lappe. I did so not because of a sense of wrongness about eating animals, but because of what I learned about the way in which we raise the animals we eat. I realized I could not in good conscience support the industrial farming system. I also realized that from my home in the concrete jungle of Hollywood, I had no access to any other source of meat, so vegetarianism seemed like the best option. *Diet for a New America*, by John Robbins, came out several years later and solidified my choice as it cites several studies showing how much longer-lived vegetarians are than meat eaters. I felt so smug in my food choices. My body, however, didn't agree with the studies. By the time I reached my twenties, I was plagued by small health issues – lack of energy and painful menstruations, primarily.

It took a full fifteen years for me to find better health and nutrition information, but it was hard for me to digest and implement that new information until I found a magazine article that specifically mentioned some of those studies cited in John Robbins' book. The article mentioned that in designing those studies, the researchers had thrown out two types of deaths: death due to suicide and death due to accident. Now on the surface, this seems reasonable, except for one thing: it means those studies were largely leaving out the impact of diet on the brain and endocrine system. Accidents are often related to poor judgement; suicides are an indication of depression and despair. These deaths are as much a function of our overall well-being as are deaths from cancer and heart attack. When deaths due to suicide and accident were factored back into the equation, meat-eaters gained an edge over vegetarians – and the gap was particularly large for vegetarian vs meat-eating women. Many women's body-minds do not fare well on a vegetarian diet. I began to change my diet in earnest that day and have never looked back. As a result, my health on all levels has greatly improved.

Part of what this experience taught me is that a purely rational approach to decision-making, using science as the only guide, is not necessarily the best approach. Modern neurobiology and quantum physics both tell us that the reality known by the rational mind is not a complete picture of reality. There is way more going on here then we can currently know through our conscious mind. In a complex and dynamic world, the pressing question for me became, *what is the best way to make decisions that will take me where I want to go?* Discovering the latest science on the human heart helped me find answers to that question that have served me well, and we will explore that science and those answers in chapter 4.

Science, like religion, can be a guide. It can shine light and illuminate your quest for healthy relationships with yourself, with the natural world, and with others. The tenets and texts of science need to be looked at carefully, however. They are not uniformly accurate. They are a work in progress. We need to question the stories that science tells us, looking carefully at their roots.

To Compete or to Collaborate?

The competition story is one of our oldest and most powerful: "You must compete to survive." Every nature program I have ever watched on TV has been laced with this story, training us to see death as life's enemy and to see eating as part of the battle for survival. It is no wonder so many are so confused about what to eat. It is no wonder that foods that are processed beyond recognition are so popular. Best not to think about what died to keep you alive. I will say much more on that subject in a later chapter, but there is a more pressing question here.

What if survival isn't the real mark?

What if our focus on survival has led us to miss what's really going on?

What if nature has a different focus?

My gardens have taught me that nature is reaching not for the survival of small bits, but for the infinite evolution of a whole. Just because humans have committed to a story that casts every plant, animal, and bacteria as combatants, does not mean that is how the rest of nature experiences it. Your body is made up of a trillion cells and 10 trillion bacteria. You are one organism composed by (not of, but by) 11,000,000,000,000 independent parts. Each one of those parts is connected to the others and is designed to perform specific tasks, but also has plenty of room for independent action. Collaboration is the name of the game your cells and your bacteria are playing, a collaboration designed to create you on a daily basis over the course of decades.

Nature is a whole system whose smaller, living parts create bigger, living parts. Cells create multicellular organisms. Many multicellular organisms create ecosystems. Many ecosystems create a living Earth. Within the systems of Earth, energy and materials are in constant circulation. Wolves and caribou are as much a whole as are your blood and bones. Survival is not the goal. Learning, growth, and evolution: these are nature's true concerns.

Are you willing to now immerse yourself in a different way of seeing and being?

Are you ready for a new story?

Could the Universe Be Alive?

I have mentioned that science is a work in progress. New technologies that enhance our perception coupled with observations that can't be explained by existing theories keep that progress happening. In Galileo's day, it was the telescope and the retrograde motion of the planets. A clearer view of the heavens coupled with the backward wandering of the planets against the background of stars – a wandering that was difficult to explain with the earth as a flat center around which all the heavens moved – led to the formulation of an alternative theory: the round earth that circles the sun. Further advances in our technologies have continued to show us the accuracy of this idea. It seems to be a good one as far as anyone can tell.

Our success with the round earth idea has helped us to believe that, overall, things are pretty much figured out; that while we are still filling in the finer details, we already have the big picture. The truth, however, is that with each keener and more finely-tuned technology we develop, the inexplicable anomalies are piling up much faster than are reasonable explanations for them. In just the past few decades we have added everything from electron microscopes and MRI scans to the Hubble telescope and Voyager probes. We can see more deeply into inner and outer spaces than ever before. The round earth theory is holding up, but many of our other current favorites are not.

The sun, for example, is a modern mystery to many astronomers. It's been almost 100 years since Sir Arthur Eddington proposed that nuclear fusion was responsible for the sun's energy. His idea was pure conjecture. He looked out in space and asked himself, "Does the sun's energy come from within or without?" He could see no source for without, but with the recent advances in nuclear technologies, he could fathom a reasonable explanation for within. His theory was published and gained acceptance, and now we all know that the sun is a nuclear reactor. Except this theory does not in any way explain the data we now have about the sun, information unavailable in Eddington's day.

Astronomers do not, for example, have a reasonable explanation for the changes in temperature that we record on the sun's surface, known as the photosphere, and in its atmosphere, the chromosphere and corona. The output of energy from a nuclear reactor, and therefore the temperatures, should be dissipating as that energy reaches the surface layers of the sun. The temperature should continue to drop as that energy travels out into the atmosphere. The nuclear reaction theory estimates that the temperature at the sun's core is a blistering 15 million degrees Kelvin (about 27 million degrees Fahrenheit). We know that at the sun's surface the temperature is a relatively balmy 5,800 degrees K. So far, so good.

The problem starts out in the sun's atmosphere. The chromosphere, the part of the atmosphere up to 2,000 kilometers above the surface, exhibits first a drop to 4,500 degrees K followed by a steady increase in temperature, rising to approximately 10,000 degrees K. The temperature then skyrockets through what is called the transition zone, eventually arriving at a robust 2 million degrees K in the lower corona. How does this happen?

It's such a little thing.

Of course, there is certainly a rational explanation.

No need to look beyond the nuclear reactor model.

Or perhaps there is a simple explanation, but it demolishes that favored theory.

The scientists of the Thunderbolts Project have an alternate explanation. These are real scientists with real degrees and real jobs at real universities. None of them are astrophysicists, however. Instead they are electrical engineers and specialists in plasma physics and related fields. They propose that our nuclear reactor explanation is a relic of an era when gravity was the most powerful force we could understand and describe. Gravity is the force that would power the sun into being a nuclear reactor. There is a more powerful force, however, that has been found throughout the Universe. This force is one we have only begun to understand and work with during the past 150 years: electricity. Think of the power in a lightning bolt. Gravity will pull you to Earth, every time, but it clearly doesn't pack the punch that electricity does.

What if electricity is the power behind the sun and stars? We use electricity for light. In fact, that was its broadest original use. Why not the stars as electrical dynamos?

As it turns out, those with an understanding of electrical engineering and plasma physics find that this idea can easily explain the temperature increase that we witness in the sun's atmosphere as well as a host of other anomalies that are not explained by the nuclear reactor theory, including faster rotation at the sun's equator, the existence and behavior of sunspots, the acceleration of the solar wind as it travels further from the sun, and the disappearance of the solar wind for 2 days in May of 1999. In this model some fusion of smaller atoms into heavier elements occurs, but that fusion is happening at the edge of sunspots and at the photosphere.

I invite you to further explore the details of this Electric or Plasma Universe Theory on your own because the full repercussions of it are stunning. Space – that 99.99% of the Universe that is called empty - becomes inhabited with charged particles (plasma) and magnetic energy fields. Plasma is an ionized gas, the "fourth" state of matter, a place where electrons roam free of their atomic nuclei. While the overall charge of such a gas is often near neutral, each unit is charged because of the freedom of the electrons to roam.

Irving Langmuir chose the term *plasma* to describe this type of gas because of the "almost lifelike, self-organizing, self-sustaining behavior" of these ionized clouds. Plasma can shield itself from intruders and isolate them in much the same way as our blood's immune system does. Plasma often exhibits a cellular structure. In fact, it is much more accurate to describe plasma as the first state of matter, given its prevalence throughout the universe. (See Scott, *The Electric Sky*, and other listings in the Resources section.)

There is one difficulty with electric stars and a plasma universe. They won't support a Big Bang. They negate the need for black holes and dark matter. They have no use for impossible objects such as neutron stars because there is a simpler explanation for pulsars. They may even debunk some or all of Relativity Theory. A Plasma Universe is a complete revamping of our current Cosmology, even bigger than rounding the earth and rotating it around the sun. A Plasma or Electric Universe is a new story and offers a new root system for our civilization.

Within the context of an electric universe, our sun shifts before our gaze. No longer an isolated mass of hydrogen and helium atoms floating in an empty and lonely void, Sun becomes an electrical organism, grazing its way through the edge of the galaxy as it eats negatively-charged electrons and spews out positive ions. It now has behaviors – the sun spot cycle and coronal mass ejections, for example. Like all living bodies, it becomes an electromagnetic signaling and receiving device moving through energy fields that convey information and offer connection to every corner of our galaxy and universe.

I have, in that last paragraph, pushed the Electric Universe theory a bit further than the scientists of the Thunderbolts Project (by suggesting that the sun is grazing), but it is a theory that does **not** automatically deny to the universe the possibility of being alive and may even offer support to such a concept. Our brains rely on electricity to think, after all, while computers rely on it to process information. Electrical forces help create the self-organizing structures that are at the core of all life-forms; they are responsible for the twisting of DNA molecules, and for the beating of our hearts. For all we know, the stars are electric, and they are having conversations with each other, and this organism we call Universe, is the equivalent of the brain of a hippopotamus hanging out in a river on a planet housed in a system even more vast than the one we see ourselves inhabiting.

Did that make you dizzy?
If it did, that's okay.
Take a deep breath.
There is so much we don't know.
Why pigeonhole ourselves into a small and meaningless existence?

A Bounded World of Fractal Infinity

The picture I just painted for you draws on a common feature of the world we live in: irregular, yet repeating patterns that move through different scales. This is the realm of fractals. Fractal geometry is a newer branch of mathematics, a non-linear branch whose complexity offers a much clearer view of the structure underlying what we call physical reality. In a fractal, the parts resemble the whole. An example from nature of a fractal is a river network. A satellite view of any river shows a repeating pattern of smaller lines joining into larger lines until the river reaches the ocean. This same fractal pattern describes the shape of trees or the form of your circulatory system. It is a pattern that effectively transports substances, either consolidating them (as in the case of the river), or diffusing them, or both (as in the case of trees and your bloodstream). Other examples of fractals are snowflakes and ocean waves, crystals and DNA.

Nature uses the irregular and non-linear shapes of fractal patterning almost exclusively in her design system, and I have found that designing food gardens in the style of fractals leads to a more satisfying experience than the traditional linear rows. Fractal patterning is much more complex. It looks more like chaos, but it is not chaos. Quite the opposite. In fractals, everything is connected and related. In discovering the geometry of fractals, I think what we have really stumbled on is not a geometry of form, but a geometry of process, or to be more accurate, a *geometry of relationship*.

I mentioned earlier that Nature does not seem interested in the survival of bits, but is greatly interested in learning, growth, and evolution. These are all processes, not things. Nature is not a thing. Nature is a set of processes, intelligent flows of energy that interact and coalesce, sometimes creating things, sometimes destroying things, but always interested in the continuation of the process itself. Nature is playing an infinite game, and relationships are at the heart of it.

A garden – or anything else – built through the geometry of fractals becomes a garden full of active processes, each connected to and collaborating with the others. This is a garden whose parts are in relationship with each other, not a garden of disconnected parts that the gardener must work to hold together. This geometry of relationship is how 11 trillion independent parts can create your body on a daily basis with remarkable consistency. You are a garden of fractals, an ecosystem, a set of processes whose motions create and support cells and bacteria. Your body is those processes in action. It is not simply a collection of cells and organs.

Another way to say this is to go back to the examples of rivers, trees, and your bloodstream. Each of these looks similar in form because each is a reflection of the same process in action, and that process is the consolidation or distribution of energy and materials. A river is a slow and consistent gathering of water from a landscape. There is a reverse distribution system possible with rivers where the materials of the ocean are gathered back and returned to the landscape. We call this a salmon run. Millions of salmon pass back up a river to spawn and then be eaten and defecated back on the land, thus distributing the bounty of the ocean to the land. A salmon run is a fractal form that the process of distribution has taken, just as the river is a fractal form for the process of consolidation.

Trees are this shape in duplicate, one above ground and one below ground. At the top are the leaves and at the bottom are the root hairs, each gathering sunlight or minerals to share with the rest of the plant. The trunk is the central channel that concentrates and allows these flows of materials and energy. Your bloodstream does the same for your body, and when coupled with the lungs, shows this same mirror image of a tree inside our bodies. The trunk, or central channel, of the aorta also contains your heart.

When we decide it is time to educate our economists in biology, ecology, and the geometry of fractals, then they will have the information they need to design a human economy that has the power to distribute essential goods and services to every person. Your lungs and heart and blood vessels have no trouble ensuring that each and every cell – 1 trillion of them – get the oxygen they need 24/7/365. In the case of rare emergencies, when oxygen is in short supply, there is an order in which it is distributed, with critical organs receiving more than less critical organs, but Nature did not choose to base the most critical element your body needs on a material in constantly short supply. We could design a money system based on fractal principles. We simply need to decide that we want to.

Look around the wild world. There is sheer abundance there. Endless abundance. This is because, mathematically, a fractal is infinite. Ask a computer to zoom in on any edge of the Mandelbrot set, a fractal structure named after the discoverer of fractal geometry, and it can do so endlessly, bringing the beautifully curved forms of the set to life.

Figure 2: Detail of the Mandelbrot Set. From Wikimedia Commons, by Maloq.

In the physical world, fractals seem to be infinite as well. Consider a mountain range. From a distance, the entire range will look like a roughly triangular object on the horizon. Fly closer, and you will begin to perceive individual peaks; that single triangle on the horizon is now dozens of individual, roughly triangular objects. Move in to examine one of these mountain peaks, and you will find that the roughness of it is the result of many smaller, also roughly triangular outcroppings. Examine one of these outcroppings, and you will see the very angular nature of the rocks and boulders which make the mountain. This process of closer examination can be continued with magnifying glasses and microscopes, and it will continue to reveal the crystalline, roughly triangular, mountain-like forms of the smaller rocks and eventually the molecules that make up the mountain. An essentially infinite number of angular molecules makes a mountain range. This is the magic of fractals. It is the process of creating infinity through repetition at every scale. (See Resources for a link to an excellent documentary: *Fractals, Hunting the Hidden Dimensions.*)

This magic shows up in a fractal garden as well. When I stopped asking how much broccoli I could grow in a season, or how much food for human consumption I could grow, and instead asked simply, "How much can I grow here?" that's when it got *really* interesting. My garden began to become infinite, because it became more complex and more diverse. It began to look more "natural." The number of creatures I can feed in a year, and still have plenty of what I grow for myself and my family, increases each year, partly because who I count increases. I feed humans, cats, dogs, goats, ducks, chickens, many species of wild birds, gophers, voles, mice, and earthworms. I feed a healthy diversity of arthropods as well as incredible numbers of bacteria and fungi. I avoid feeding deer, but it invariably happens once or twice a year for a few days when they find their way past the fence, so I feed deer too. My garden has a boundary, but what happens inside that boundary is infinite. I only need to look more carefully, zooming in with computer-like magnification skills to find that infinity.

You, like my garden, are also a bounded infinity. You are a natural phenomenon of fractal beauty. Zoom inside your own body and, as mentioned before, that singular you becomes 11 trillion cells and bacteria. Zoom inside those and you find even greater numbers of molecules, then atoms, then atomic particles, then sub-atomic particles. Science has been searching with great vigor for the foundational particle, the smallest thing in the universe, but there seems to be no end.

Nassim Haramein introduces this concept of a bounded infinity in his video, *Black Wholes*. Every piece and part of the universe has boundaries, yet within the context of those boundaries the further divisions and magnifications are infinite. Universe is divided into multicellular galactic clusters and then cell-like galaxies. Galaxies are divided into more cell-like groupings, including solar systems. Solar systems contain planets. The diversity of planets seems amazing because this is where we first get to a scale that we can see and relate to well. On Earth, the division of ecosystems into organisms is massive, which returns us to the level of the multicellular creature and its component cells. We may not be inside the brain of a hippopotamus in a universe much more massive than our own, but it is not impossible.

Your brain is one of your most fractal features. Housed inside a skull of set boundaries, the neurons of your brain have an infinite ability to branch, like a tree or a river. Albert Einstein allowed his brain to be autopsied after he died. His brain was not larger. It was not heavier. It had no more neurons by number than the average human brain. What it did have was more branching. Einstein's neurons had patterned themselves into dendrites (a tree-like, branching form) to a much greater extent than is normally found. Einstein had found a way to magnify his brain power, somehow encouraging his neurons to grow into a finer and finer pattern, like the root hairs of a plant, creating connections with each other, learning, sharing, communicating, creating a garden of dense relationship. Our brains are one of the best examples of a structure with the potential to be infinite even though it is bounded. Perhaps that has been Nature's intent for us all along.

Let that sink in for a minute...

We have explored a vast terrain in this chapter, and you may be wondering how it can be useful to you. Does it really matter what powers our sun? Of what practical use is a bounded infinity in your everyday life? To answer the first question, I suggest talking to every geek and energy nerd you know about the possibility that the sun is an electrical dynamo. When I first read about this possibility, I was reminded of the work of Nikola Tesla. Tesla was a genius far ahead of his time. His work with wireless electrical systems may have been based on an intuitive understanding of the amount of plasma in our universe and of the powerful magnetic fields flowing in the cosmos. With this new story of an electric universe, is Tesla's work now reproducible? I imagine it is.

As for the usefulness of knowing about and thinking of yourself as a bounded infinity, I invite you to play with this Playtime exercise:

Playtime! An Infinite Breath

Breathing is the most essential thing we do. Supplying oxygen to all of our cells is critical. When we are amply supplied with oxygen every part of our body-mind benefits. Our cells have all the energy they need to do the things they do, including moving, digesting, or thinking. Most pathogens and diseases have a hard time surviving in a high-oxygen environment. Breathing fully is our first daily medicine.

When I was first learning about bounded infinities and fractals, I happened to take a voice-opening workshop. A good portion of this workshop was devoted to teaching us to breathe because our instructor, Dolli Melaine, had found that very few of her voice students knew how to breathe well. She had us do many exercises designed to open and expand our lungs, particularly in the back and sides.

In working with one of these exercises, I found myself lying on my back, thinking about fractals and infinities. As I did so, I shifted out of focused consciousness into a relaxed state (the extra oxygen was already working), and the next breath I took felt, well, infinite. I swear it could have gone on forever. The image that accompanied this breath was of an infinite array of tiny lungs lining the surface of my lungs, each one filling and then opening into another tiny array of more lungs, and on into infinity.

I have no idea whether or not the cells or structures lining the lungs look like lungs or not, but at the process level they are lungs, and you have billions upon billions of them. We are capable of some very deep breathing. I will not try to take you through a full range of exercises here, but I would like to offer you this simple practice:

Start with a yawn. Yawning is deep breathing at its natural best. As you yawn, use your awareness to notice what your body is doing. What areas of your belly and ribcage expand? What happens with your neck and jaw? Do you feel any muscles anywhere in your body that relax as you yawn? What do your chest and shoulders do during the inhale? What do they do during the exhale?

Yawn several times, using each one to notice what is happening in your body as you do. Be curious, and pay some special attention to the feelings in the back and sides of your ribcage.

Now, lie down on your back with your knees bent and your feet flat on the floor. Put one hand at the base of your ribcage, where it forms that upside down U over your diaphragm. Let your neck be long as you lie on the floor. Breathe, noticing if and how your hand moves with the breath. Let your mind's eye be just below your hand, inside your ribcage. As you inhale, watch from inside as your chest opens and expands. Feel your lungs as they drink in this air. Relax as you exhale.

Continue to play with your breath, feeling the sensations of it with your attention in the area of your diaphragm. Relax. Notice if there is any area of tension in your chest or ribs. If so, let your next inhale move gently toward this area, then let the tension begin to ease with the exhale.

When you feel done with exploring your breath, stretch and sit up. Yawn once more and notice if anything feels different. Has your mood changed? Are there any new sensations in your body? How does your chest feel? There is no right or wrong here. The goal is simply to notice what is.

You can do this exercise as often as you like, and I would encourage you to try it several times a day over the course of a week. As you move into and out of this exercise, you can remind yourself of your infinite nature. Think of all the many cells lining your lungs that receive this oxygen, taking it into your blood. Be open to any imagery that comes to mind. You might see a flower opening, hear the wind rustling through pine needles, or feel a river running through you. Whatever you experience, be curious and interested. Notice, and let it go.

Three

Collaborative Intelligence
Drives Evolution

The bounded infinity housed in your skull is an amazing structure, one that I now picture as an infinity of roots reaching deeply into the pre-physical soil of consciousness. Because it is so complex, we tend to think of intelligence as arising from our brains, but does it? The heart is increasingly being described by neurobiologists as a brain in its own right, something we will look at more closely in the next chapter. The gut is also beginning to receive the designation of brain, making us three-brained, not single-brained, creatures.

The more we discover about body chemistry, including hormones and neurotransmitters, the more the entire body looks like a mind, if not a brain. Numerous organs, including the heart, manufacture hormones, which impact the thought processes of the head-brain. The microbes housed in our guts can also manufacture brain-altering substances. For example, they participate in creating and moderating the levels of serotonin in our systems. (Serotonin is a potent neurotransmitter linked to feelings of happiness.) The entire body ecosystem contributes to what happens in all of our three brains. This is what has led to the emergence of the more complete concept of the body-mind, a continuum of body-wide processes that affect our thinking, our behaviors, and our health.

This new understanding of the body-mind has also led psychologists to describe different forms of intelligence. Intelligence is no longer as simple as a high IQ. There is now emotional intelligence, musical intelligence, naturalistic intelligence, kinesthetic intelligence, social intelligence, and other recognized forms of what we call intelligence.

Why does intelligence matter here? Because "intelligence" is a critical part of our current story-root. How we think about intelligence colors our relationship with ourselves and the world around us in profound ways. What you learned about your own "intelligence" from teachers and family members will influence the choices you make in charting your life's path. When you think of your heart as a "dumb and emotional" organ needed to move your blood around, it is easy to dismiss it and to disregard the messages it sends to you. Likewise, if we believe the world around us to be empty of intelligence, then it is easy to dismiss its interactions with us as meaningless. It becomes difficult to understand the language used by all other forms of life for conversation, because we have become convinced that verbal languages arising from the head-brain are the only way to communicate.

J. Allen Boone described this best in his book, *Kinship With All Life*. The book tells the marvelous tale of Boone's adventures one summer as a caretaker for the dog, named Strongheart, who played Rin-Tin-Tin in the silent film era. Theirs was not an easy relationship. The dog was opinionated and headstrong (or intelligent and able to think for himself), and his way of seeing the world was very different than Boone's. At first Strongheart's intelligence was not appreciated by his caretaker. It took several weeks for Boone to come to appreciate the dog, but when he did he began to wonder, *how was it that Strongheart could understand him so easily, yet he could understand the dog only with great effort on both their parts?* For example, Boone might be working in his study, pause for a moment and think about taking the dog for a walk, and Strongheart would be up and bounding to the front door. However, if the dog wanted to go out for a walk, it often took several attempts at communicating his desire before Boone could understand the request.

One warm afternoon, Boone sat on a bench overlooking a view of the Pacific Ocean with Strongheart at his side. He felt calm and relaxed, and his mind wandered back to this question of how to better understand the dog. Immediately, he saw an image of a large tube extending between himself and the dog. With himself standing above the dog, his thoughts and communications rolled easily down the tube to reach Strongheart. However, with gravity working against him, Strongheart had to work very hard to get communication to roll back up the tube to Boone. The flash of insight that accompanied this image was Boone's realization that his attitude about the dog's intelligence was what made him higher than the dog. It was the firmness of his belief in his human superiority that placed him on a pedestal, putting him out of reach of much of what the dog had to share.

Boone quickly realized that when two creatures saw themselves as equals, the tube would be level, and it would be easy for communication to flow in both directions. He also realized that to see himself as inferior to another would invert the tube, putting him at the low end and making it difficult for him to talk with the person "above." This is one of the biggest difficulties with hierarchical structures in human societies. The people at the top are often much restricted in their ability to receive communication. Much to his credit, Boone took this lesson fully to heart, coming to embody an openness and light-heartedness that allowed him to make friends for three days with a vibrant fly he named Freddy.

If flies can become our friends, what about trees and plants? What forms of intelligence do other living creatures hold? How can we benefit from what the rest of the living beings on this planet know, given the lack of common verbal language? It all depends on how you perceive the landscape of intelligence and your relationship to it.

The Merriam Webster dictionary defines intelligence as "the ability to learn or understand or to deal with new or trying situations." Most living creatures fulfill this definition pretty easily. Even bacteria have had the intelligence to outwit our antibiotic onslaught of the past half century, developing superbugs that are outwitting us in hospitals around the country. Who hasn't seen a tree, knocked down by a snow storm or other encounter, that nonetheless continues to grow toward the sun? Clearly all of nature can deal with "new or trying situations." That's why we are all still here.

I have my own understanding of intelligence, one that demands a little more of all of us. I define intelligence as *the ability to promote processes that foster the infinite evolution of fractal forms of life.*

Let yourself think about that for a moment...

This is an intelligence that creates sustainable systems; systems that keep needed elements cycling freely and abundantly through all the planet's many parts. These are the intelligent systems that circulate and clean our air and water, that keep nutrients such as nitrogen and phosphorus circulating in our soils, and that foster balance among all these many moving parts. This is the intelligence that creates multi-cellular creatures (mini-ecosystems) as well as larger ecosystems. This is the intelligence that connects our planet to a living, plasma-filled universe.

This is also the intelligence housed in every atom of Nature's body, as each *thing* interacts with the world around it, engaging in the relationships that give it solid form. Intelligence is not a rare commodity in the natural world. Intelligence is part of the nature of the world. As we learn to recognize and then respect this intelligence, we will learn to use the strategies that create sustainable systems. Even better, we can learn to use strategies that create ever evolving, learning, and growing systems.

Life Seeks Balance Between Opposites

More than anything, the intelligent processes of life seem to be a balancing act, an engagement with duality that requires the careful blending of two opposites. Cell biologists report that our cells have two modes of operation: they are either growing or defending. To grow means to be openly taking in food, exchanging information with the environment, and doing the work for which the cell is designed. To defend means to be closing the gates of the cell membrane, monitoring the environment carefully, minimizing any exchange with it, and pausing in the work for which the cell is designed in order to conserve needed energy and resources. Because defense is a disconnection from outside resources, it is also a step in the direction of dying. For cells, there is no stable, static, mixed or in-between phase, only the choice of growing or defending. The balancing of these two activities creates the life of every multicellular creature on the planet, including you.

Your cells spend a good portion of their time regulating the levels of potassium, calcium, magnesium, and various forms of sugar in your bloodstream because this balance is critical to your functioning. The oceans and forests of Gaia have regulated the levels of carbon dioxide, methane, oxygen and other gases in the atmosphere to create a balance that has maintained a consistent set of climates around the planet for millennia. Healthy ecosystems remain healthy through a delicate balancing of predator and prey populations. Too few wolves means too many caribou. This causes overgrazing, erosion and nutrient loss from the ecosystem - and an eventual die-off due to starvation among the caribou.

Because life on Earth is predicated on duality, life embraces both sides. Like a person riding a bicycle whose muscles must make constant micro-adjustments in order to remain in motion, so too must life make constant adjustments, aiming always for that midpoint between the two sides of a duality, finding stability, but never able to find a static place between. Life is in motion for the same reasons that a bicyclist is: to stop means to end the ride.

Stability and change are a pair that life seems particularly adept at embracing. Each day is different, and yet it is similar enough to the day before to give us a sense of stable continuity. This is because while the material components of the world are in constant circulation (change), the relationships between those components are more fixed (stable). The sun is constantly streaming new particles in our direction, yet we rotate around it at a set pace and distance. You take in new oxygen, food, and water every day, renewing the materials that compose your cells, and yet the cells themselves maintain the same set of connections or relationships with each other.

Balance is intimately tied to relationships that are collaborative. Whether your cells are engaged in keeping blood sugar levels in the proper balance, utilizing the oxygen that just came in via the lungs, mounting an immune system response to that tiny sliver in your index finger, or any of the other multitude of balancing actions going on in your body as you read this, there are at least a trillion little ones – cells – working together to be you, to be the body-mind system that is reading these words right now.

How do our cells do all that they do? How do they communicate, synchronize, orchestrate, and integrate the hundreds of processes going on inside of you at any given moment in time? Are cells automatons, little machines that respond only in set ways to the environment around them at the behest of their DNA? Given the number of "new and trying situations" they encounter every day, that seems unlikely. The emerging science of epigenetics, meaning "above the gene," is discovering that many genes in our DNA can be switched on or off. This switching is affected by the outside environment and can even be determined by our attitudes and thoughts. The effectiveness of placebos is evidence for the impact that our thoughts have on our DNA and the switching on or off of genes.

Throughout the sciences, the mechanistic model is being usurped by a synergistic network of collaborative, self-organizing, living systems. Our bodies and cells are one such self-organizing system, and I suspect that far from being automatons, our cells are imbued with a decision-making power grounded in a holographic sensitivity to higher order balance. Possibly through their connection to the morphic field, cells are imbued with the intelligence needed to make decisions that keep the larger organism in balance, and that means that they are imbued with the abilities they need to have in order to collaborate with one another.

There is no tick-tock machine with set outcomes at work in this world. There is only life with her repeating fractal patterns, playing her infinite game, exploring every avenue and every possibility, always with an eye to more complexity and diversity, using evolution as the pathway to a never-ending experience of being. Competition is not the main player in this story; collaboration is.

Discovering Our Collaborative Foundation

Our culture's favored story about the natural world is that it is a competition free-for-all with only the fittest surviving. This story is grounded in two beliefs. One is the perception of life as something that is opposed to death, rather than of life as a singularity encompassing death and relying on death to keep the balance. It is also based in the belief that life is limited in scope and is fundamentally scarce and fragile. Putting these two elements together leads to the conclusion that the only way to maintain life is to survive, and that survival will require constant and vigilant competition. Fortunately, none of that is true. There is a small but growing cadre of ecologists, biologists, and other scientists who began to examine this fundamental assumption about competition at least 40 years ago. Their work is rewriting everything we thought we knew about how Earth works, starting with the smallest pieces: the bacteria, fungi, and cells that form the foundation of everything we call living.

In the beginning, on Earth, were the bacteria, or to be more exact there was something scientists long thought was bacteria but that is now named *Archaea*, a new kingdom of organism that is older than all the rest. The archaea thrived on ancient Earth because they eat ammonia, hydrochloric acid, and sulfur, preferring environments that are low in oxygen. Close on the heels of the archaea came the beings we still know as bacteria, a huge array of tiny microbes with the power and intelligence needed to invent such key features as bodies with tails or photosynthesis, the digestion of sunlight into sugars and carbohydrates.

It is now believed that at a pivotal point 2 billion years ago, an archaea merged with a swimming bacteria. Perhaps the archaea ate the bacteria, and the bacteria survived, or perhaps it happened some other way, but the end result was the first multicellular creature, an amoeba or an algae, the kind of thing we call "pond scum." It was a beneficial relationship for both creatures. The bacteria had more protection from the harsh environment as well as from its predators; the archaea became more mobile.

This was not the only merger to happen; it was simply the first. A billion years later, an oxygen-breathing bacteria merged with the amoeba and became the precursor to every animal and fungi alive today. A third merger occurred 700 million years later when a cyanobacteria, a photosynthesizing bacteria, joined the ménage to create the precursor to all plants. This process of creation is called *symbiogenesis*, the creation of new forms of life through the creation of symbiotic, or mutually beneficial, relationships.

We have seen that *things* are created at the quantum level through the interaction of awareness with energy. Now we are learning that even at a larger scale, *things* as organisms are created through interactions or webs of relationships, and the vast majority of those relationships are symbiotic, mutually beneficial, and collaborative. Every *thing* that you see, every living *form* that exists, is there because of a mostly hidden set of *relationships*. You can function because of the collaborative relationship of your cells with each other and with your microbiota. A tree does all that it does because of the collaborative relationship of its cells with each other as well as with fungi and other living creatures of the soil. All multicellular life is built on a solid foundation of collaborative relationship. This is the fundamental process driving life's evolution on Earth.

I do not deny that competition exists. It does play a key role, for it is our troubles and problems that create the impetus for change and growth, and that trouble often arrives in the form of a competitive relationship. Competition stimulates the need for evolution, but the long-term, stable solution to that need lies in the creation of new and collaborative relationships, not the destruction and elimination of competitors.

Necessity is, indeed, the mother of invention. The need for new forms results from the need to create new relationships in order to solve a problem and regain balance. Oxygen-breathing bacteria were invented because the invention of photosynthesis had destabilized the atmosphere of our young planet, putting so much oxygen (a byproduct of photosynthesis) into it that Earth's early life forms were being incinerated by flares of spontaneous combustion. Cyanobacteria needed a complementary partner, a relationship that would create balance for life's respiratory needs to be met.

Long-lasting and stable forms are based on collaborative, symbiotic relationships.

Pause here.

How does your body feel as you reread that bold sentence above?

Does your breathing change?

Does your posture shift?

What is your body's experience of that thought?

This understanding explains why the goal of sustainability is so unreachable for our sophisticated and technologically-advanced civilization. It does not matter how many solutions we have at our fingertips – and we have plenty of them in every field from building to agriculture to education to energy to money systems. We will continue to find it difficult or impossible to implement those solutions so long as the foundation of our society is based in legal, economic, educational, and political systems that enshrine competition as the inevitable and primary form of relationship.

Outside the family structure, we are continually taught and encouraged to survive competitive relationships. For some people, the same competitive lessons apply within the family structure as well as outside it. There are few of us who get any significant education in creating collaborative relationships with others, and almost never with the world beyond the human. If we want sustainability, if we want a society that works in harmony with the natural world, then we must learn the fundamentals of building symbiotic, mutually-supportive relationships with soil, plants, animals, and insects as well as other people. Fortunately, that knowledge is available to us; it is modeled for us by the world around us – if we allow ourselves to see – and it is even built into our genetic material.

Nature Collaborates at Every Level

Microbes can do the things that they do because they share and collaborate with ease. The DNA of a microbe is a fluid thing, not a fixed and little-changing blueprint. Bacteria are known to copy and share their DNA with each other as though at an orgy. They have no need for patents or other forms of information protection. When one solves the riddle of how to survive a dose of antibiotic, it shares that information with every other microbe it meets, whether it is of the same species or not. In fact, the concept of species is becoming increasingly difficult to apply at the level of bacteria. Any one individual within a species may have as little as 40% of its DNA in common with other members of what we have deemed to be the same species.

Collaboration and cooperation extend beyond the realm of the microscopic and well into the realm of the larger world that we see every day. The four species of nuthatch in North America are an example of nature behaving cooperatively. These are birds with the habit of traveling along trunks and branches of trees, sometimes hanging upside down while seeking out insects or seeds. In forests where two or more species coexist, they tend to divide the territory. The Red-breasted Nuthatch favors oaks and other deciduous trees, leaving the conifers to the White-breasted Nuthatch. In some instances, they have even been noted to divide a tree with one species eating in the upper canopy while the other keeps to the lower branches. Rather than go for head-to-head competition, they have branched and diverged enough to get along, adding more to the fractal infinity of the forest.

Forests are places of collaboration in other ways as well. While we are often told that the trees of a forest are competing for scarce sunlight by fighting for a position in the upper canopy, new technologies, such as radioactive gases, allow us to trace the movement of molecules through a forest and show us that something very different is going on. Trees feed each other. Cover the canopy of one tree with a dark cloth, cutting off its ability to photosynthesize sunlight, and sugar molecules made in other trees – even from different species – will show up in the covered tree.

How could this happen? Trees in a healthy forest are connected underground by many miles of fungal mycelia, a one cell thick network of living tissue that occasionally explodes aboveground as a mushroom. One teaspoon of healthy forest soil can contain a half mile of fungal mycelia. Through their roots and their alliances with the fungi, trees are in constant communication with the forest whole. Think of this fungal network as both an internet, conveying information, and as a superhighway, conveying goods and services. Fungi trade minerals, water, and organic compounds to trees and other plants in exchange for the sugars made through photosynthesis. Trees convert enough sunlight to sugar to feed not only themselves, but also their ecosystem.

Another example of collaboration at the macroscopic level comes from agriculture. There is a very old story about the damage done to crops through competition as the plants in a field have to compete for scarce sunlight, nutrients, and water. This is why farmers and gardeners alike are taught to prefer monocrops, fields or beds devoted to one species only. Gabe Brown, a regenerative farmer in North Dakota told a very different story in a presentation at the 2016 Nevada County Sustainable Food and Farm Conference. He described for us a study examining the benefits of cover crops in which he had taken part. Cover crops are plants that are used to build the health of the soil in between cash crops. They come from many different plant families including the nitrogen-fixing legumes, the fibrous-rooted grasses, and the all-purpose brassicas.

In Gabe's study, ten different cover crop species were being trialed, including radish, mustard, hairy vetch and others. Each species was planted in its own plot. With seed and ground still to spare at the end of planting, Gabe decided to add an eleventh plot that contained all the remaining seeds, mixed and sown together. This study was conducted in North Dakota with no supplemental irrigation. It happened to be a very dry spring and summer with only 2 inches of rain falling. In all of the first ten plots, the seeds germinated, then dried out and died. Gabe's slides showed us the remains of small, dried-out plants resting on the soil surface. The slide of the eleventh plot looked very different, however. Here was a picture of riotous green plants at least 2 feet tall and in many shades and textures. The mixture had not only survived; it had thrived where its component parts could not. Collaboration enabled both survival and reproduction of all ten species.

In *The Soil Will Save Us*, Kristin Ohlson says, "Weirdly, we've all been schooled in the notion that plants are takers, removing nutrients from the soil and leaving it poorer. But when plants are allowed to work with their partners in the soil, they're givers." This same idea applies to ourselves as well. We've been schooled in the notion that humans are inherently selfish takers. However, when we are allowed to live in healthy relationships with our own non-human partners, it turns out we are givers too.

Collaboration Within Us

The collaborative nature of the world around and within us is a discovery that we are making anew in every field of science on a regular basis. Gastroenterologists are discovering the absolute necessity of bacterial species to the healthy functioning of the human gut. The bacteria in our guts can digest things which the cells of our bodies cannot. This means that we can access a wider range of nutrients because of these microscopic allies housed in our bodies. Immunologists are discovering that these same gut microbes educate our immune systems, helping our bodies to know the microscopic details of the environment that we inhabit. Allergies are now being tied to damage done to our gut microbes through overuse of antibiotics, extreme sanitation, and lack of access to healthy soils.

When the Human Genome Project got underway in 1990, scientists expected to find 100,000 protein-coding genes in human DNA. Instead they found 20,000-25,000, not much more than in a mouse. We are a complex species, and we do make use of a vast array of proteins throughout our bodies, so where are the missing genes? As it turns out, the bacteria have them. The cells in our bodies are outnumbered by bacteria by a factor of 10. The DNA in our cells is outnumbered by the DNA in bacteria by a factor of 100. For every strand of human DNA in your body, there are 100 strands of bacterial DNA, and the bacteria use this DNA and the information it contains to our benefit. People with a healthy microbiome – a diverse array of the microbiota we evolved with - are at less risk for diabetes, cardiovascular and liver diseases, and cancer. They are also at less risk for a host of autoimmune diseases, dementias, and autism.

Our bodies are designed to operate as ecosystems, with a wide range of different species collaborating to create health and well-being for us throughout our lives, but our microbiota do need some assistance from us. Some of this assistance is built into our DNA. The third most abundant class of molecule in human breast milk is a very complex carbohydrate called Human Milk Oligosaccharide (HMO). HMO is so complex that infants cannot digest it. As any nursing mother knows, it takes a large amount of energy to make breast milk. Why would we be designed to put so much precious energy into making a substance that our babies cannot use? The answer is that the infant's developing gut bacteria – their microbiota – need this carbohydrate. It feeds the Bifidobacteria, a species that is essential in helping the developing child to thrive. HMO is also an essential food for Bacteriodes, a type of bacteria that plays a big role in helping the baby to digest solid foods. The presence of HMOs allows the gut to be seeded with Bacteriodes, so that it is present and ready to get to work when solid foods first arrive.

Collaboration with the natural world is designed into the cells of our bodies. If we hadn't been so brainwashed by the mindset of our current culture, we would never have forgotten what we all learn as kids: it feels better to get along. We wouldn't have lost sight of the truth all around us: many individuals pulling together create far more than do separate individuals fighting and squabbling.

Playtime! Meet and Greet Your Cells

This is a simple exercise I like to use as I am going to sleep at night. I think its simplicity belies the powerful effects it has on enhancing the environment you create for your cells. The researchers of the Heartmath Institute have shown that people in a relaxed and coherent state – something we will talk about in detail in the next chapter – have the ability to wind and unwind their DNA. You can influence your cells and their behaviors, for better or worse. This is a practice that shifts your influence in the direction of better.

Lie on your back, and take a moment to breathe deeply. You can yawn or use some of the breathing practice from the last playtime if you like. Close your eyes, and allow a wave of relaxation to flow through your body starting at your head and moving down through your feet. Let this wave of gentle energy pull tension from your muscles, causing them to relax. Breathe.

Let your attention move to the inside of your body. Imagine all the little and intelligent cells that are creating you. All the cells that are your heart, lungs, and liver. Imagine these organs as composed of many, many dots – living and moving parts of you. Let your awareness scan your body, becoming aware of all these little lives within you. As you do, say hello to them with your mind. Thank them for all that they do. Thank the cells of your heart for beating, and the cells of your brain for thinking, and the cells of your kidneys for filtering your fluids. Let yourself and your cells be bathed in appreciation for all that goes on in your body.

When you have said your final thank you, let yourself drift off to sleep. Notice in the morning if you feel any different than usual. Did your cells respond in any way?

As I have learned more about the essential role of bacteria and microbes in my body, I have started to include them in this exercise. I notice and thank them as well for helping to create me. They seem to appreciate it as much as my cells do.

Four

Your Heart is Not a Pump

Your heart maintains a rhythmic beat. Millions of pacemaker cells within it, entrained to each other, pulse out a beat that is both steady and highly variable from one moment to the next. The pulsing, squeezing rhythm of your heart helps to move your blood around, but your heart alone is incapable of moving blood throughout your sixty thousand miles of veins and capillaries. The heart's beat also sets the pace for the pulsing squeezes that your veins and capillaries perform. These little tubes are alive as well, and they constrict in a spiraling motion that maintains blood flow.

The Doppler imaging that helps us to see Earth's weather systems is also helping us to see the flow of blood in our bodies. Your blood does not flow in a single current. It flows as two streams, circling around each other – like the double helix of DNA – creating a vortex and a vacuum in your veins.

The other organs of the body, kidneys and liver, for example, also squeeze. The expansion and contraction of your muscles squeezes the veins as well. All of this is needed to move two gallons of blood through your body in each minute, oxygenating every one of your trillion or more cells. It is true that if the heart were located outside your body, the stronger ventricle, the left side, would have the strength to pump a stream of water 6 feet up into the air. However, that is the least of what your heart does. It is so much more than a pump that to describe it as a pump is one of our biggest errors.

If you watch the body language of the people around you, you will notice that the majority of us gesture toward our chests, right at heart level, when we speak about or refer to ourselves. In spite of all our thinking, that sense of self is located much more strongly in the heart area than it is in the head or the brain. Nonetheless, we generally don't trust our hearts.

I spent many years searching for answers to life's challenges and deeper questions with only my brain. My parents and family preferred this approach. My education in a college-prep high school fostered and encouraged this approach. My professors in college encouraged this approach. A few years after college, I became a member of a spiritual group that trained us to access our intuitive abilities by staying in our heads, avoiding our hearts like the plague. Everyone seemed to agree that the heart was overly emotive and unreliable, while the reasoning brain could and would lead me to health, wealth, and happiness. The only problem was that wasn't how my life was working out, and I don't see it working out that way for most people.

Who is that self that we are pointing at when we gesture toward our chests?

We have many theories about the creation, evolution, history, and purpose of human beings. They cover the gamut from divinely-made-and-then-ostracized to completely-accidental-and-purposeless. These are the same theories that teach us to perceive ourselves and the world in ways that create the Behemoth. Changing my understanding of my own heart was the key for me, the key that unlocked the door into a larger, deeper, and more loving reality filled with unlimited possibilities. The biology of the heart organ is phenomenal. The heart is not a pump. It is an organ which perceives and organizes, leads and guides, knows and cares.

The heart lies at the center of your upper body and a bit to the left. This organization indicates both its central role in your body-mind, as well as its affinity for and connection to the right brain. The right brain controls the left side of the body. It synchronizes that part of our awareness that is wholistic, intuitive, creative, and spontaneous. The right brain is a parallel processor, capable of handling many millions, if not billions, of bits of information per second. The rational and logical left brain is a linear processor. It handles about 40 bits of information per second. Your heart is aligned with a brain that can handle staggering amounts of information on a moment to moment basis.

The heart is one, divided into two. There is one heart but it has two sides, two pulses. One side collects depleted blood from the body and returns it to the lungs. The other side collects oxygen-rich blood from the lungs and sends it out to the cells of the body. Duh, Duhm. Duh, Duhm. Duh, Duhm. The heart has an in breath and an out breath. A yin side and a yang side.

Each pulsing beat of your heart generates an electrical charge, measured at two-and-a-half watts. This electrical output is what is being measured on an electrocardiogram. As the blood enters and exits the heart, it travels in a vortex – a fast spinning, spiraling tornado. As tiny, charged particles in your blood – ions – move into this vortex they produce a magnetic field. Coupled with the electric field generated by the pulsing of its cells, your heart produces an electromagnetic field that extends well beyond your skin. This electromagnetic field is much stronger than the field created by the brain. The electrical part of this field is 20 times stronger than the electric field of the brain. The magnetic part of this field is 5,000 times stronger than that generated by the brain. Electricity is yang. Magnetism is yin. The heart is two-sided, but it has that strong connection to our intuitive, yin experience.

The heart's electromagnetic field acts like any other electromagnetic field: it carries information, and it interacts with other fields, receiving information in the process. It's as though you have, housed in your chest, both a radio broadcasting station, putting out that signal 24/7, as well as a radio receiver, translating energy waves into a language your body-mind can understand. This broadcast ability is broad-band. It happens across a wide range of the energy spectrum. Your heart is constantly broadcasting information about your health, your emotional state, and your intentions. When you step into a room full of strangers and instant-ly notice the "vibe," you are using your heart field to read the other heart fields in the room. It's automatic.

Our ability to measure this field of the heart with technological equipment is very recent. Until just a few decades ago, we did not have technologies sensitive enough to find these heart fields, so scientists as-sumed they were not there. Now we can measure them to a distance at least 10 feet beyond the body. That is as far as our instrument sensitivity extends. The field of the heart is assumed to extend much further, and scientists now make this assumption because they have discovered that while biological organisms are not sensitive or reactive to strong mag-netic fields, those same organisms are very sensitive to fluctuations in very weak magnetic fields, much more so than are metal or silicon-based devices – the basis for the devices that are used to measure the heart-field.

Living creatures do not care much if there is a strong magnetic field around, the type that will move iron filings about. Put us near a weak field, however, and our hearts are all ears. It helps to notice those subtle changes in the heart-fields of your spouse or child, and they are noticea-ble to you because you have a heart.

The Earth, like yourself, is surrounded by a weak magnetic field. As it changes and fluctuates our bodies notice this as well. The heart is the central processor of this information. It can do this because it is not just a muscle, it is an integral part of your nervous system. Sixty percent of the cells that are your heart are neural cells, exactly like the cells that make up your brain. The heart is now considered by many neurobiologists to be a brain in its own right. It is an intelligent part of our body-mind. It has the capacity to process the information it takes in, decide what actions to take, and respond accordingly, often without any need to consult with the verbal and rational side of our conscious awareness.

In his delightful book, *The Secret Teachings of Plants*, Stephen Harrod Buhner says, "Analysis of information flow into the human body has shown that much of it impacts the heart first, flowing to the brain only after it has been perceived by the heart. What this means is that our experience of the world is routed first through our heart, which 'thinks' about the experience and then sends data to the brain for further processing." This can happen because the heart has direct connections to several of the brain's centers including the amygdala, thalamus, hippocampus, and cortex. These connections have no gates, no on/off switching. Your heart and your brain are in a constant dialogue.

Your heart influences your brain, and your entire body, in other ways as well. In addition to being part of the nervous system, your heart is part of the endocrine system. The heart makes and disperses at least five different hormones. These hormones circulate through the blood system, influencing kidneys and other organs in ways that regulate blood pressure and other body functions. For example, one of these hormones, called atrial natriuretic factor (ANF), can stimulate your kidneys to increase the excretion of sodium. The same hormone also binds to receptor sites in your eyes influencing ocular pressure and focus, creating either a sharper focus or a softer, more peripheral focus. Your heart has a hand in every part of your experience, including your perceptions.

The heart's hormones also influence the brain. Brain natriuretic factor (BNF) is also secreted by the heart and helps to protect the hippocampus and therefore plays an important function in both learning and memory. ANF can alter the brain's production and release of a host of hormones including cortisol and dopamine. Dopamine is an essential neurotransmitter facilitating the flow of information from neuron to neuron. Lack of dopamine is implicated in Parkinson's disease. The heart is also able to make its own dopamine and secrete it into the bloodstream to circulate through the body.

Your heart is a leader in regulating the entire function of your body. Each beat sends a pressure wave through the body. This pressure wave is picked up and answered by the squeezing of the other organs and the veins and capillaries as they circulate your blood. Your heart reads these returning pressure waves, making minute adjustments in the timing and strength of each beat. These adjustments in turn influence the amount of hormones, ANF especially, that circulate in the blood. Your heart listens carefully to your body, hearing each cell, and adjusts its actions accordingly.

Much of the information that your heart receives both from your internal environment and your external environment is also processed in the brain, but is never sent specifically to the left brain for what we think of as conscious processing. Signals may nonetheless reach the left brain. "Notice this person." "Stay away from there." "Go left now." This is often the format of those intuitive hits that make it to conscious awareness. Intuitive signals, those communications emanating from the heart, may also take the form of emotional signals. There is a tremendous amount of nonverbal information and communication encoded in the experience of feeling "good" or feeling "bad." Rather than dictate that information out in lengthy book format, thereby missing an opportunity because of the slowness of left brain processing, our hearts send us quick hits of densely-coded information.

Because our heart is more closely aligned with our less-verbal right brain, and because it needs to process millions to billions of bits of information per second much of the heart's information and decision-making processes reach our conscious awareness only through these very subtle signals. This is what we call "intuition." It is a knowing that we hold, but can't explain where it came from because the processing never happened in the rational part of the brain. The knowing pops into rational awareness, fully formed, but we have no idea what signals or information came along and what logic determined this new idea, inspiration, or knowledge. This is why it is so easy to dismiss intuition as unfounded or unreasonable. Intuition is never unfounded, nor is it unreasonable. It is impossible, however, to trace the process that brought it to your rational awareness.

The Heart as Leader of the Nervous System

The brain is a pretty cool tool. Unfortunately, our hyper-focus on it has left us blind to the power and intelligence housed in our hearts. We have been taught that the brain in our head is the best leader of the body-mind, yet our bodies function better and maintain a higher degree of health when the heart gets to set the pace and tone for our body-mind systems.

Every organ in our bodies is a biological oscillator, sending out an electromagnetic frequency. The heart is by far the strongest of these, with the brain and gastrointestinal tract also generating strong frequencies. The other organs of your body, as well as each cell, also oscillate. Their signals are far weaker, but they are there. A healthy body displays a high level of resonance among all these different oscillators. Like a drum circle of seasoned practitioners with everyone displaying entrainment to the basic rhythm even as they play with extra, faster beats or fewer and slower beats, the cells and organs of a healthy body match and play off each other in the practice of creating you. This is called coherence.

Let's play for a minute. Take a moment right now to notice your breathing. No need to judge it in any way, just feel the passage of air into your nose and down into the chest and/or belly. Notice the feeling of expansion in any or all of these areas, and then notice the feeling as the air passes back out. Now listen for a minute. If it helps you to focus, you can close your eyes as you ask yourself: What is the farthest away sound that I hear right now? What is the closest sound? How many sounds do I hear? It is not necessary to name each sound, simply notice them. Notice your next breath again. Feel it as it happens.

Do you feel different now than you did when you started this simple exercise?

Whenever we take time to focus inwardly on our body, especially on the breath, or whenever we take time to focus with interest and curiosity on the input of the five senses, our heart rate slows and we begin to experience a change of state. If you continue in this, a cascade of changes will happen throughout your body causing your heart to become coherent with itself. The cells of the heart will synchronize with each other more strongly. The other organs and cells, the other biological oscillators of the body, including the brain, will then begin to follow the lead of the heart. You will have strengthened your heart-field, and your body will become more coherent as a result.

Coherence equals health for the simple reason that more can be accomplished when everyone pulls together. Greater harmony leaves more room for both subtlety and complexity. A heart that experiences a high level of coherence is actually more variable in its beats and rhythms. Heart rate variability is one of the markers now used to measure the health of a heart. With all the information being processed by the heart, with all the body processes that it needs to balance to keep the symphony that is you going, the ability to vary its beat in small, subtle and numerous ways is key to a job well done. When we place the lion share of our daily attention on the brain and its activities, we neglect our hearts. We neglect to provide opportunity for strong coherence to develop, both in the heart and in the entire body. Heart rate variability declines, and the aging process begins.

Heart rate variability is a fractal process. It is one of the ways the heart becomes a bounded infinity. It is one of the ways the heart becomes more without moving outside the boundary of its cell walls. More variability means more information is being processed and used, more possibilities are being explored.

When the brain grabs our attention, when its signals set the pace for the body as a whole, including the heart, we spend more time activated in the sympathetic nervous system. This means we spend more time in "fight or flight" mode with more cortisol pouring through our systems and more activation of stress. When the heart has our attention, everything slows down. (Did you feel it start to happen with that last sentence? It did for me, even as I wrote it.) The parasympathetic nervous system gets activated. The beat of the heart slows. Relaxation occurs. The eyes begin to dilate, and focus softens. Learning abilities increase in this state. A wider range of the neocortex comes on line. We can think more clearly. Yes, even our brain function improves when we allow the heart to fulfill its role as leader of the nervous system.

This central role of the heart in the nervous system is knowledge that is embedded in nature's web of intelligence. The Hawthorne tree, *Cratageus*, is a renowned heart herb and has been for thousands of years. It is also a powerful herb for the nervous system. This is not by chance. This is because hearts are the natural leaders of the nervous system. To treat one is to treat the other. The heart sits at the center of our bodies, leading the beat of the circulatory system, holding space for the flow of information in the nervous system, gathering communication from every cell in your body, collecting the information encoded in electromagnetic signals from outside your body, and making adjustments in response to all of it.

The heart sits at the center and a little to the left, accessing billions of bits of information in every second: Deciding. Responding. Guiding.

Journey with Hawthorne

The drum is beating just a few feet from my head in the steady tempo used for shamanic journeying. I am finding it to be both annoying and distracting, a part of the pressure I feel from inside to make this a "real" experience.

I am at an outdoor herb workshop on Hawthorn Medicine, taught by one of my favorite herb teachers and mentors, Heather Luna Keasbey. The assignment is to journey into a Hawthorne tree and ask what medicine it has for me. We are already a few minutes into the assignment, and my mind is jumping around. I feel very much in my body and not on a journey.

I hold in my mouth a ripe, red berry from the tree, and I decide to eat it. As the soft-textured, mild, apple flavor touches my tongue, my teeth find the hard seed inside. One seed. Very hard. I think about being in this seed and getting planted. I imagine the feel of the cool dark earth that surrounds us, and the slight feel of pressure and love as the gardener's hands press the soil from above. I can feel that she rises. Then water trickles and flows around me, and we drink.

I feel the root tip form and swell, emerging from the seed casing to explore the soil as it digs downward, knowing without hesitation what direction is down. After a while, a shoot forms and begins to push upward, feeling a sense of urgency as it travels through dark until – suddenly – there is light. Light! I feel joy at the finding of the sun's rays.

Now my rational mind kicks back in, analyzing, as it jumps through its store of knowledge about tree and plant growth. As my seedling grows quickly into a tree, my attention is drawn to the flow of sap and I watch, knowing in my rational mind that it will be traveling, like the blood in our veins, in a spiraling vortex as it moves from leaves to roots, roots to leaves.

I realize I have never asked the question, "What medicine do you have for me?" My attention continues to be drawn only to the sap flowing. Now I notice the ease with which this living fluid travels in the aboveground parts of the tree and then into the below ground parts. I notice how different these two halves are, almost as though I am watching two trees – or two chambers creating one tree. It was only later, in retrospect, that I saw the heart in its guise of tree. At the time I noticed more the metaphor of the flow of energy from the visible physical to the invisible, non-physical and then back, like a breath. I recognized a desire to have that much ease and clarity in my own connection to the soul-side of me.

The information my heart took in during this journey was dense and vast. Revisiting it in quiet times has yielded more and more rational-level understanding. It didn't matter that my mind wanted to get in the way. My heart did its work, storing for me a wealth of understanding, waiting patiently for those gaps in my day when I was relaxed, and it could add to the download.

The heart is a very special two-sided organ, one that allows for a flow of information from the unseen world to the seen world, from the energetic to the physical, from desire to action. As the strongest oscillator in our bodies it is likely a part of our connection to the human morphic field, allowing for the impressions made upon us by our experiences to flow back to this repository of vibration and information; then translating them into new growth. The heart is a doorway to the world of wholeness, a world where consciousness is the soil on which matter grows and where human curiosity holds deep creative power. The heart is one of our most nurturing roots.

Playtime! Heart Connection

I am often asked how to know when to listen to your heart. When do you follow its guidance, and when do you listen to your rational mind? I am certain that the heart is never wrong. It is always best to listen to it. If you feel concerned about trusting your heart, however, then you are likely having some trouble with signal clarity. Are you getting a clear reading of your heart's communications or is your rational mind stepping in and giving you a fuzzy reading, doing its best to masquerade as your heart?

This is a common problem because of the training we are exposed to throughout our school years and adult life, to disregard anything that cannot be pinned down through rational logic. People speak of some ideas as being "counter-intuitive," but they are talking about the quick calculations of their rational mind, not the intuition of their heart. For example, after a lifetime of training in hyper-sanitation, such as is practiced in American society, it may seem "counter-intuitive" to eat some dirt for your health and well-being. This is your rational mind masquerading as an intuitive, and not your heart speaking to you.

The exercise included here is to strengthen your connection to your heart as well as to develop its coherence. It will help you to learn to know when you are receiving a heart communication and when you are hearing your left brain interrupt or "translate."

Find a comfortable and relaxed position, either sitting or lying down. Begin by closing your eyes and noticing your breathing. Watch as the air travels into and then out of your lungs. Notice if you are breathing into your belly or into the sides and back of your ribcage. If not, gently ask your body to take a deeper breath and allow more oxygen to enter.

Pick a spot on your forehead, and imagine that you are now breathing in and out of that spot. Watch as the air gently fills your head before it travels to your lungs and then returns the same way. Take several breaths in this way.

Next, notice your shoulders and allow your next breath to enter from them. Let your shoulders become permeable, allowing your breathing to pass through on its way to and from the lungs. Repeat this for two or three breaths.

Now notice the palms of your hands and allow them to receive the air as you breathe. Imagine little openings in your palms that gather in air as you breathe, and then release it. Repeat this for three breaths.

Then notice the soles of your feet. Allow your breath to enter through your feet. Feel it travel up your legs and into your chest before returning to release out your soles. Repeat this three times.

Notice your hips next and allow your breath to enter from two points, one at the crest of each hip bone. Allow this oxygen to circulate freely in your pelvis as well as in your belly and chest, and then exhale it out through those same two points in your hips. Repeat this three times.

Notice now your heart. Allow your breath to enter in at your heart, then gently exit. Take another breath through your heart. Notice your heart breathing, then notice it beating. You are welcome to place a hand over it, if this helps you to feel its beat. Watch the rhythm of your heart beat for perhaps a minute. Thank it for doing this for you. Notice what feelings you have as you focus now on your heart. Notice, and let it go. Ask your heart if it has a memory it would like to share with you. Notice if anything comes up, and then return your attention to your breath.

Take a deep breath, stretch and move around. Notice how you feel right now. Is your mind calm or active? What emotions do you feel? What does your body feel like? Is anything different?

I suggest doing this exercise daily for a week – or more. As you develop your skill in heart connection, you may simplify or alter this exercise in whatever way your heart guides you to do so. If no memory arises during the exercise, let it go. Chances are at some later point in your day, when you are focused on something else, a memory will surface and you will wonder why you are thinking about that. This is your heart opening the channel of communication with your left brain. Notice it. Celebrate it. (Dark chocolate? Time out for a walk? A high five with your partner?) Appreciate yourself for your willingness to open to your heart.

Five

Nature is a Nervous System

A tree does not need a heart organ because it is a heart. It also does not need a brain organ because it is a brain – or, more accurately, it is a fully functioning and complete nervous system - perceiving, processing, and responding intelligently to the information gathered from its surroundings. This is true of all plants. Plants and trees do not have nervous systems. They are nervous systems.

This is an idea that was inconceivable just a few decades ago, but is now being explored and supported through several scientific disciplines including plant ecology and the new field of plant neurobiology. In the PBS documentary, *What Plants Talk About*, plant ecologist Dr JC Cahill of the University of Alberta asks the question, "Do plants have behaviors in the same way that animals do?" Most people would dismiss this question without a second thought, but Cahill took the time to look. He used time-lapse photography to study the movements of plants and their roots and the results are stunning. A radicle emerging from a seed moves in circles, looking exactly like a snake or a worm sniffing the air. When the growing root discovers a rich cache of nutrients, its growth slows as it stops to feast, much like the pattern of movement demonstrated by a grizzly bear as it roams a landscape, slowing or stopping to devour berries as it finds them.

We also now know that plants are rapid learners with good memories. This was clearly demonstrated in a laboratory by Dr Monica Gagliano of the University of Western Australia and Dr Stefano Mancuso of Florence University. The team worked with the Sensitive plant, *Mimosa pudica*. This is a plant that closes its leaves when touched. By using a specially-designed apparatus that "dropped" the plant 15 cm, giving it a jolt but not threatening its well-being, the researchers were able to "condition" the plants – in the same way we get conditioned to something that at first seems novel, like a loud noise, but that is then ignored as we realize it holds no threat or interest.

Just 4 to 6 sudden drops, repeated within a few seconds of each other, was all it took for the Mimosas to begin to stop closing their leaves. After a full day of the experience, the plants were ignoring the drops completely, with their leaves remaining fully open. Some of the plants were given the sudden drop treatment once again 6 days later. Many did not close their leaves at all, remembering their earlier experience perfectly. Those that did close their leaves on the first drop stopped doing so by the second or third drop. Even after a further 4 weeks off, the Mimosas remembered their training and kept their leaves open when once again dropped.

Plants are also sophisticated and creative chemists and communicators, chemistry being one of the main forms of plant language. Some scientists prefer the term "signaling" over "language" when referring to plant communications, but the end result is the same: exchanges of meaningful information with other living members of the plant's community. The chemistry in a plant's body is not static. It is produced as an intelligent response to or interaction with the other members of the environment.

One example of this is the evidence we now have that shows how plants have trained deer and other browsers, such as goats, to nibble only a few leaves and then move on. Plants can and do change their body chemistries in as little as 3 minutes. When a deer comes along and starts to eat the leaves of a toyon bush, for example, that bush will increase its production of tannic acid, making the leaves much less tasty. The same bush will also create a volatile chemical that evaporates into the air and is received by the surrounding plants. This chemical tells the neighbors that browsers are nearby, and they begin to increase their production of tannic acid as well. A deer that spends a few minutes chowing down on one plant will not only get a heavier hit of tannic acid, but by the time it moves on to the the next bush, it will have to eat that same heavy load of tannins there as well. The pattern that wild browsers seem to "naturally" use - take a few bites here, a few there, and keep moving - is a pattern that reflects what they have learned by staying in one place too long. It is a pattern that allows deer to participate with their plant allies in creating a healthy and balanced ecosystem.

Plants also recognize sibling and other kin relationships. The work of Dr Suzanne Simard of the University of British Columbia is especially revealing when it comes to understanding plant relationships. Using radioactive Carbon-14 gas, she was able to track the transfer of carbon from one tree to others. Mother trees do feed their young, nurturing them as they grow from the forest floor into the canopy.

Simard also describes the aboveground forest that we see as being only one third of the forest community. Two-thirds of the living forest is below the soil surface and includes a fungal component that is massive. Like the bacteria in our guts, these fungi act as allies, working with the trees to find minerals, make needed chemicals, retain and transfer water, and share information. Forests are organized, community networks whose individual trees are dependent on maintaining good relationships with a wide variety of "others."

When it comes to plants, the nagging question for scientists is often, "How?" How do plants process so much information when they have no nervous system, no neurons, no brain? I think this question arises because we are looking at things backwards. We have begun by assuming that intelligence is predicated on the existence of brains, yet life requires intelligence. Nothing survives without the ability to sense its environment, integrate the information it gains from those senses, and respond accordingly. What is interesting is that in order to become mobile, animals had to compartmentalize what plants, in their rootedness, simply experience as part of themselves.

The word *dendrite* means "branched like a tree." Dendrites are the part of the neuron that conduct electrical messages. We name our active brain-parts after trees. This is not a coincidence. Both animals and plants use the same fractal structure that allows information to flow freely. Our evolutionary leap was not in developing a process for working with complex levels of information; the leap was in discovering how to carry around a structure for doing that while feeding it, protecting it, and nurturing it. We did not invent intelligence. We are simply, and beautifully, another form of it.

A Network of Intelligence

A map of the internet looks remarkably like a map of our brain neurons; it also looks remarkably like a map of the fungal mycelia in a healthy forest soil. Consider how much information is traveling through the internet every moment of every day. Your brain, with its combined linear and parallel processors of left and right hemispheres, is processing at least that much information on a moment to moment basis as well. Knowing that fractal structures reflect the processes they perform, it seems reasonable to assume that the mycelial network of the forest is processing a similar quantity of information as well.

There is another structure that also resembles a map of the internet. For decades now, astrophysicists have been discovering a filamentous structure to the universe. The pictures arriving from the Hubble space telescope show us a network of lines, made up of plasmas, called Birkeland currents, that fill intergalactic space. Galaxies have fractal, information-sharing structures throughout their bodies. We do indeed live in an intelligent universe.

The entomologist, Dr. Phil Callahan, is the person who first taught me to appreciate the subtler aspects of intelligence in the natural world.

His work with radar during World War II caused him to correlate insect antenna to radar antenna and explore the abilities of insects to read the electromagnetic waves of their environment. He found that sick or diseased plants emit an electromagnetic signal that calls the "pest" insects to them. Food is the best service a sick plant can offer to its ecosystem as its reproduction is likely to be faulty. Using electromagnetic frequencies to call in insects is another way in which plants communicate with their ecosystem.

The hidden fields of the electromagnetic spectrum are common in nature. I say hidden because we cannot see or hear these waves with eyes or ears – at least the majority of us seem not to – but they are as real and present as the signals that feed our cell phones and WiFi systems. When I walk through a forest, I look at the antenna-like shapes of the trees around me, all pointed at the cosmos, and I wonder, *what are they receiving?* Are they taking in signals from far distant stars, or even distant galaxies? What conversations might these trees be having with our sun? Are they reading the whispers of the wind and alerting the fungal mycelia to coming rain or tornados? What do the trees know as they gather in billions of bits of information from this universal system?

I look at the many different species of tree, the differences in shape and leaf structure. Pines and firs are tall and straight, with fine needle-like leaves. Perhaps they are the ones designed for deep space reception. Oaks and deciduous trees are more open and umbrella-like. Perhaps they are designed for reception of the news from our solar system and atmosphere. The information gathered is certainly shared with the fungal mycelia, and thus the rest of the forest and ecosystem. Does it go any deeper? Do the rocks with their crystalline structures gather this information as well and convey it deeper into Earth?

As I was preparing this manuscript for formatting, I discovered that the Heart Math Institute is currently conducting research into the electrical nature of trees, finding that the trees of a forest are connected in this way as well as through the fungal mycelia. In fact, changes in the electrical output of trees may be useful in predicting earthquake activity because these changes in the trees reflect changes in the rock below. We are embedded, like cells, in an interconnected, fractal, living system, one that uses electricity and magnetism to share and process information at every scale.

We are also discovering that water has information gathering and transferring abilities. Homeopathic remedies have been used for hundreds of years now and are surprisingly effective given that the making of these remedies involves diluting the original infusion (be it from an herb or a piece of metal or something else) in increasing amounts of water. Science has not yet found an explanation for the mechanism that allows these remedies to heal illness, but water seems to somehow gather and focus information from the substance it is exposed to during a careful process of succussion, or sharp shaking. This information is then transferred to the body's cells and nervous system in a way that allows the body to respond and heal itself without producing side effects.

Water, like rocks, is a crystalline substance, one that conducts electricity quite well. Salt water, such as our blood or ocean water, is an especially good conductor. What nervous system functions might the oceans be performing on this planet? What hidden networks exist in those vast depths? We know very little about these possible qualities of the oceans; however, I see a hint of what we may eventually come to know in recent discoveries about whale song. We have known for a long time that whales sing - at least some species including humpbacks and blue whales. Recent examination of these songs has revealed both beautiful symmetry and a completely unexpected level of information-density in them. A half-hour of whale song reveals the equivalent in information to that contained in *Moby Dick* – the novel about a white whale that weighs in with a whopping 663 pages in some of the latest editions. Imagine how fast you would have to speak to convey that amount of information in a half-hour.

Connect and Restore

My husband owns a bookmark with a quote by Henry David Thoreau: "I believe that there is a subtle magnetism in Nature which, if we unconsciously yield to it, will direct us aright." Flows of electrically-charged particles create magnetic fields, with weaker flows creating subtler fields. The heart is part of that subtle magnetism in Nature. Earth's field is part of that subtle magnetism. The plants and animals around us also put off subtle magnetic fields which are processed through your nervous system. These fields are all part of the working of Nature's nervous system. They are our connection to Nature's nervous system and to the information and wisdom contained there.

When your emotional balance is off kilter, what's your first choice for help or relief? Whatever your answer may be, if you have the option of going outside to a quiet place among trees or out to some more wild place, does that help? Would that suffice even?

I have had my own bouts with depression, and I experienced a particularly long and nasty streak during the "midlife crisis" of my forties. On the outside I made sure I looked functional and fine, but on the inside I was often caught in a swirling maelstrom of uncertainty about my purpose in life as well as a deep inner criticism of my past actions and life circumstances. This kind of thinking is obviously not helpful, and on a few occasions I found myself contemplating suicide. When the suicidal impulses became strong, I would instinctively reach for a stable connection to nature's nervous system - a tree - preferably a large, older tree.

There is a large, old Black oak that grows in a quiet, lower corner of my homestead. It has seen fires and lost large branches, but it continues steadily on. I would seek out this tree and sit with my spine against its trunk. My sessions with the tree usually started with bouts of crying and complaining, but eventually, as some of my excess angst got released, I would find myself sitting against the tree breathing more deeply, finding the inner space to shift my attention from me to the tree. I would feel its rough bark pressed against me, supporting my back, and I would begin to imagine the flow of sap underneath. My mind would quiet a bit. Tense muscles would relax on their own. I would find more space between thoughts, and the feeling in that space was one of calm. As I continued to keep most of my focus on the tree behind me, I would continue to feel better and more at ease in my body and mind. My nervous system would begin to match the tree's nervous system, and healing was able to happen in that quiet and calm place.

Sometimes on these visits I had big aha's and useful insights. Sometimes I got up simply feeling better, able now to move through my week with more self-acceptance. The decision to visit the tree was not a decision of my rational mind. The decision to visit the tree was most often made when that mind had given up on me, and my heart-mind became free to guide and direct me. Eventually I learned to go before it got that bad. I learned to let the instinctive, calming heart-mind guide me into connection to nature's body-mind and knowledge.

The Care and Feeding of the Human Nervous System

This modern world is very hard on the human nervous system. Bright lights and light at all hours of the night are just two common features of modern life with which we did not evolve. Add to this our immersion in systems that require 40 hours or more of seriousness, called work, each week as well as the constant threat of loss fed to us through the daily news, and we have created the perfect recipe for stress.

The problem with stress is that it impacts your body in many unhealthful ways that contribute to high blood pressure, insomnia, and other precursors to disease. From a nervous system perspective, stress activates the "fight, flight, or freeze" syndrome, which means that it activates your sympathetic nervous system. Contrary to the name, the sympathetic nervous system is not an empathic place. When it is activated, the older, "reptilian" part of our brain gains the upper hand, while the younger neocortex is impaired in its ability to think rationally. It doesn't matter whether you are a janitor or a stockbroker, stress impairs your brain function, reducing your capacity to perceive and conceive of the many possibilities and opportunities that may be right in front of you.

The complementary side, the balancing partner, to our sympathetic nervous system is the parasympathetic. This is the system that remains calm and relaxed and empathetic, thinking clearly and seeing multiple options in every situation. Digestion and sleep are improved when the parasympathetic nervous system is operating, making it very good for your health. Optimally, we would spend the lion's share of our lives with the parasympathetic system operating in our bodies, using the sympathetic system only occasionally for dangerous or emergency situations. Unfortunately, the Behemoth is designed to encourage us to use our sympathetic system as much as possible.

The Earth, however, has a natural resonance, or vibration, called the Schumann resonance. This is a global background frequency that vibrates at 7.8 Hertz, which is in the region of alpha brain waves, the frequency of meditation or daydreaming. This resonance occurs because, "Believe it or not, the Earth behaves like an enormous electric circuit." (Quote from "What is a Schumann Resonance?" at nasa.gov.) This resonance is part of wild nature's restorative powers. It assists us in activating our parasympathetic nervous system. It assists us in feeling good.

Take a breath here, and notice your body right now. Notice how it feels. Now imagine the last time you were in a wild place, preferably someplace far from roads and cell phone reception. Close your eyes and let your body remember the sounds around you, the feeling of the wind or sun on your skin, the colors that you saw. Breathe, and let yourself be immersed in that place.

How do you feel now? Has your breathing changed? Is your heart rate different? Immersion in nature, even through your imagination, is one of the surest ways to activate the parasympathetic nervous system.

Playtime! Nurture from Nature

For this exercise, you will want to find a plant or tree for which you naturally feel an affinity. It is not important if it is a large oak or cedar or a small potted thyme. The first plant that springs to mind is probably your best choice.

Begin by sitting near this plant, and taking a few minutes to practice what you have learned already. Breathe, and then breathe again, letting your breath deepen. Notice your heart and its beating. Close your eyes and notice what you hear, then what you smell, then taste, and then feel. Breathe.

When you are ready, open your eyes, letting them remain relaxed and unfocused as you begin to take in this plant. Slowly, look at it more closely, noticing the color of the leaves, the shape of stems or trunk, the textures of it. Lean close and sniff it, taking in the molecules of its volatile chemistry. Brush it gently with your fingers to feel its textures. Let yourself be interested in this plant. Breathe.

Return your attention to yourself for a moment, and notice how your body feels. Are there any areas of your body that draw your attention? Has your mood shifted at all? What thoughts are running through your mind? Simply notice these things, and then return your attention to the plant.

Imagine that this is a wise being sitting with you, one with an unshakable connection to nature's stable nervous system. Imagine the invisible lines of its electromagnetic field touching the invisible lines of your heart-field. Allow your heart to absorb whatever information it needs in this moment. Breathe.

When you feel done, offer your gratitude to the plant. Thank it for connecting with you. You can offer it an exhalation rich in carbon-dioxide as part of your thanks.

Take a moment to stretch and notice how you feel. Is anything different? Again, there is no right or wrong here. Just noticing what your experience is will lead to any changes your body-mind system needs.

Six

Life is One Whole

One of my favorite books as a young twenty-something was Richard Bach's book *One*. There is a moment in that book that I will never forget, a mind-altering and re-ordering moment for me, a word that hit me like a ton of bricks and caused goosebumps to rise on my skin. In the book, Richard and his wife, Leslie, are flying in their small plane. They have somehow passed into a timeless place and are flying over a vast landscape, a fractal pattern that extends infinitely in all directions. This pattern reflects all the potentials, all the multiple directions of every life lived. It's the pattern of all those "what if" possibilities, lived out side-by-side. It is all the ways your life could have been had you gone to that school instead, kissed that boy or girl, taken that road instead of this one. But not just your life, everyone's lives, laid out in a fractal pattern of gigantic and beautiful proportions.

Bach is taking in this pattern as he talks with a guide that has arrived with this new territory. She has magically appeared in the back of the plane's cockpit and is offering advice on how to use this opportunity to explore the many potential realities of Richard and Leslie's lives. Awed by the vastness of this patterned landscape and by the immensity of the lives laid out before them, Richard asks, "How many lives are there?"

His guide seems taken aback for a moment, surprised by the question. She looks at him with curiosity before replying very simply, "One."

The Many Forms of One

There is a plant that lives in the desert southwest of North America called wild tobacco or coyote tobacco, *Nicotiana attenuata*. Coyote tobacco blooms at night and is pollinated by hawk moths, *Manduca spp.* Hawk moths make it possible for coyote tobacco to make seeds and reproduce, but at a price. The moths also lay their eggs on the plant. These eggs hatch into the caterpillar known as the hornworm, a voracious herbivore well known to gardeners who often find them feasting on beloved tomato plants. Too many hornworms can decimate a strong stand of coyote tobacco, so the tobacco plant has devised options. One of those options is to feed the hornworms the equivalent of a sugar pill, a sweet nectar that is produced on the hair of the plant's stems. This sugar pill causes the hornworm to put off a strong smell, one that draws lizards and other caterpillar predators to come to the aid of the plant.

Another option that the coyote tobacco uses, but only when the hornworm numbers have become overwhelming, is to change its flowering. Over the course of a week, a plant that was blooming at night will begin to bloom at dawn instead. The shape of the flower is also changed, as is the smell and chemistry of the nectar. These changes draw in hummingbirds and allow them to pollinate the tobacco instead. Because hawk moths are no longer being called, no new eggs are laid by the hawkmoth, and thus the hornworm population is reduced. Here is a plant with many options, yet why would coyote tobacco have continued to choose - over hundreds of thousands of years - to preferentially bloom at night for the hawkmoth?

In the competitive, life-versus-death worldview, this choice makes absolutely no sense, and scientists find it puzzling. Why not just shift to only blooming for hummingbirds? Wouldn't a competitive evolutionary

process have mandated this? What could possibly explain the plant's re-
fusal to behave or evolve in this way?

Take a breath for a moment here. Let your awareness include your
breath and your heart. What if Bach's guide was right? What if there is
but one life in all the Universe? What if coyote tobacco and hawk moth
are a connected unity, now divided into two – a rooted part and a mobile
part? What if in the coyote tobacco's experience, it is not separate from
the hawk moth, but merely distinct from the hawk moth – in the same
way that your liver is distinct from your stomach? Would its choice to
bloom for the hawk moth now make sense?

If the coyote tobacco, the hawk moth, and the hornworm are different
aspects of one being, then we are now looking at the beautiful story of
how one superorganism feeds its different parts while producing enough
of those parts to assist in the maintenance of an ecosystem. The coyote
tobacco, in giving stinky sugar pills to its caterpillar-part, is contributing
to the health and well-being of lizards and birds. It is behaving as an essential part of an ecosystem, and may experience itself as distinct but not
separate from that either. Coyote tobacco chooses to feed the humming-
bird only as a means of balancing its relationship with its hawk
moth/caterpillar self, for balance is an essential aspect of life, as we have
seen.

I am not suggesting that the moth evolved biologically from the tobacco or vice versa. I am suggesting that there is a deeper relationship
there, one that smacks of entanglement and unseen connection within the
soil of consciousness that creates this physical reality. The coyote tobacco-hawk moth superorganism is one of those anomalies pointing us in
the direction of a different worldview. It is an example of nature's organizational wholeness as distinct and living cells create distinct and living
organisms. We do not yet have a specific term for the more complex
"superorganism" exemplified by the tobacco-hawk moth partnership, but
this is the next stage of organizational wholeness. This stage then leads
into ecosystems.

As we are discovering in the forests, ecosystems are made up of a complex of organisms creating one body, a community of distinct parts, but not a collection of separate parts. An oak tree emerges from the soil and lives for centuries rooted in relationship to that soil. Every falling leaf is a recycling of fertility to that same soil, food for the millions of micro-creatures who have come to live there as well. Without soil, the oak tree could not exist, and without the oak tree, the soil could not evolve into the complex and living being that it becomes when in relationship to an oak. Are the two really separate?

I am certain that as our perceptual abilities expand (whether through technology or the cultivation of our heart-minds or both), we will continue to validate that ecosystems are communities of connection creating an even larger organism, Earth. We have a name for that organism, one that acknowledges the living, intelligent nature of our planet: *Gaia*. This is an organism of whom you are a part.

The Many Parts of You

We now know how essential bacteria and microbes are to human life. They are the foundation on which we stand, and the new term describing this complex of species that are a part of each and every human body is the *microbiome*. The microbiome in your gut – or lack of it – determines the health of your brain and your immune system as well as the effectiveness of your digestion. Seeing into the microscopic world has shown us how simplistic our concept of a "multicellular" organism is, for without the complex of species that work with your cells, you could not function effectively.

How separate are you from the world outside your skin? How would your life change if you decided to accept that some bacteria are part of what you call you?

I once had a job working in the produce section of a large health food store in Virginia. I usually worked the evening shift, which meant making sure that the fruit displays - the apples and pears and oranges - were full and looking beautiful for the morning shoppers. A dark-haired, tough-looking guy named Bruce was often my coworker on that shift. Bruce was also interested in the meaning of life, and we enjoyed many exceptional conversations during our shift.

I remember late one evening, about an hour before closing, I was stacking the deep-red Empire apples on the corner display, while Bruce was working on the green Granny Smiths nearby. It had been a good conversation, and while I don't recall what Bruce had just said to me, I can still clearly feel the click that happened inside. Whatever he said caused me to change. I took a deep breath, and felt a sense of wholeness and connection that was new and different. I took another breath, watching myself breathe, and I said to him "Wow, like, when does the air become me?" He gave me a questioning look. I continued, "Is it me when it passes into my nose? Does it have to get into my bloodstream? Does the cell have to use the oxygen and then it's me?" He laughed and then added, "And when does the carbon dioxide stop being you? When it leaves a cell? When it enters your lungs?" I smiled. Exactly.

Where does your life end and the life of the planet begin? Are they separate or are they part of a vast continuum of One Life, endlessly individuated into smaller and smaller parts? Your body is infinitely connected to all that is "outside" it. Air. Soil. Water. Bacteria. Fungi. Plants. Trees. Animals. People. Planet. Sun. Stars. Galaxies. Universe.

Embracing Death

Life, in my cosmology, is a singularity. Like the heart, it is one organ, but it has two sides - or two chambers. We name those chambers birth and death. Birth and death are part of the one, unopposed process called Life. Life itself has no opposite. It takes both birth and death to create and sustain and balance the process of life.

I know that statement may be hard to swallow because it is an ingrained belief throughout Western cultures that life is rare and difficult and that we are all barely hanging on by a thread. Life is so often framed as the struggle against death. Life requires survival, and survival means fighting and struggling in whatever way is called for to avoid the abyss of death.

Gardens have shown me a different perception, a different relationship to death. The cycle of the seasons brings a constant parade of births and deaths into my yearly experience. The flush of new growth in the spring as seeds germinate and the world becomes clothed in many shades of green is always an energizing experience. The first hard frost of fall and the sight of withered pepper and tomato plants might bring some sadness as the season of bounty comes to an end, but it also brings relief as it signals a time of rest and the opportunity to start again, try new strategies, and create the garden anew.

The death of a plant is the opportunity to reclaim its carbon and other nutrients for other life forms. Earthworms, arthropods, fungi, and bacteria will use the plant to foster their own life. They in turn will feed other creatures, including other plants, or create humus – the ultimate in stable and life-creating soil. Death in a garden is simply the cycling of molecules and energy. There is nothing life-ending and permanent about it. In fact, it is an essential component in the balancing, dynamic processes that make life an endless, infinite experience.

How would your life be different if it was framed not as a temporary and ultimately futile struggle, but as a flow from unseen to seen and back, like the flow of sap from the roots of a tree to the crown and back? What if life is a never-ending dance of energy and consciousness into material, bounded form, and then back into non-material, unbounded, non-form? What if this process of life creates an ever-expanding reservoir of knowledge that we all contribute to through our experiences? What if this reservoir of knowledge, this morphic field, is that thing we call intelligence that can't be pinned into any one part of any body or brain and yet seems readily available as we deepen our perceptual abilities?

I invite you to take a deep breath here. Drop down into your heart. Connect with its field. Ask your heart's opinion on this matter.

Reframing Our Story About Life

You have new tools now. You know that you can connect with your heart and its vast field of information. You know how to connect your nervous system with nature's and gain access to even more vast fields of information. Information by itself, however, is useless without a frame to give it meaning – or useless when the frame being used is inappropriate. The frame creates the context for how one piece of information can relate to another. You have had a heart all your life, but you may not have seen it or experienced it as you do now. You may have been afraid to trust that "over-emotional pump" in your chest, because that frame of "pump" could not encompass the possibility of your heart as a knowledgeable, intuitive, and guiding partner.

A heart that sits in the frame of "electromagnetic oscillator and brain" becomes a very different organ. It has new possibilities and is capable of having much more complicated relationships. It gives a whole new meaning to the word: *heart*. I have offered in this chapter a new framework for life, one that is bigger than the usual frames I hear. To help you consider this new frame, I want to share another story, a story about an experience that helped me to reframe my understanding of life.

I felt both sad and injured the day my dog, Trinity, died. She was only six-years-old, and her death came upon us over the course of just a few days, leaving a gaping hole in my home and in my chest. Trinity was the first dog that I called "mine," but it was a mutual choice. She was a black and tan, Queensland Heeler/Kelpie cross, and I trained her to herd sheep and goats with me. She trained me, with calm patience and utter persistence, to let her sleep on our bed. She knew her place, and she helped me to learn it as well.

Trinity had a quiet dignity that impressed many who met her, including the vet tech at the clinic that performed her spay operation. I was waiting to pick up Trinity that afternoon, when the young tech, a woman, called me aside. She looked at me with a direct and serious gaze and said, "This is a very special dog." I nodded in complete agreement. She held my gaze as though making sure I knew this before she would agree to give Trinity back to me. "She is a very special dog," I affirmed with equal seriousness. Only then did she take me to get my dog and give me the post-op care instructions.

My husband and I both tended toward a belief in reincarnation at the time of Trinity's death, and so amidst our grieving, we spoke hopefully of her return. Loving friends told us immediately about a litter of puppies. They were 7-weeks-old at the time of Trinity's death, and also Queensland crosses. One stood out in the pictures they sent us, a black-and-tan puppy. I was cautiously interested, but I wanted my Trinity back. I wanted to continue the journey that we had begun together.

There were signs. My husband got a Chinese fortune that said, "It's ready, go pick it up." I had dreams. In one a golden retriever pup, fell into a pool, her head dipping under water. I yelled from the shore to Tom, my husband, who was right at the water's edge. He reached in and grabbed her up. She lay still for a moment and then jumped up, fully alive. In the dream, I felt so much joy and relief, yet that dream confused me for a while because I had no desire for a retriever in the family. In retrospect, it is easy to decipher: Retrieve-her.

The dream that gave me the reframing I needed came a little later. I had entered a beautiful garden. I knew this garden. It was not mine, but I worked in it sometimes. I was happily weeding a vegetable bed, when a woman came running up to me, completely distraught. There was a problem with a very special fruit from a very special tree, the only one of its kind. The tree was called the Bishop's Lemon. I felt no distress or concern in the dream. I took the woman's hand and led her to the tree and showed her how healthy it was. I showed her the new fruits, already well-formed for the next crop, hanging on the tree. We gathered up the spoiled fruits that lay on the ground and took them to the compost.

Waking from that dream, I considered something I had not thought about before. I thought about the idea that a soul could be more like a tree, with its many connections and many simultaneous fruits, than it is like a single fruit. Reincarnation might not be as simple as one lifetime after another. It might be a more complex and simultaneous unfolding. My dog had died, but she had not left me alone and abandoned. There were many other fruits on her tree.

Three weeks after Trinity died, circumstances conspired to deliver me to the black-and-tan puppy's home. I found myself stuffed into the cab of a pickup truck along with my husband and our friend, Tabor, and our remaining two dogs, Rose and Zorro. A bull calf in the back, under the camper shell, completed the party. We were delivering the calf to the puppies' owners as a favor. It was a four-hour ride.

When we arrived, I saw seven little pups lined up on the porch, barking at our truck. I was tired and stiff and could see nothing remarkable about any of them. The Shorthorn dairy we had arrived at was a patchwork of pastures, with cows in several directions. We took a walking tour with many of the puppies following along. I still wasn't sure that any of these was a puppy for me.

When we returned to the house porch, I sat down at ground level. A rush of puppies came up to crawl on me and lick me. The black-and-tan was not among them, but after the others had left, she did come up to me. She sat down next to me, without jumping up on me. She looked up at me. Then she lifted a front paw and put it gently on my thigh, saying in the exact way that Trinity had so often said, "You can love me now." I did so, and let the tears flow.

Trinity and I have continued our journey together, she just has a different name now. Her death changed me. It broke my heart open, and I am a better friend to her now because of it. She is different too. Some of the things I had wished for Trinity are in her new form. She is more athletic, more gregarious with children, and not at all prone to car sickness. A body was shed as Trinity hit the refresh button, but her life never ended. Life is never-ending, and when we reframe our relationship with death, perceiving it as a necessary component of life, we also reframe our relationship with life, creating the possibility of a richer and deeper experience.

The Key Ingredient to a Continuing Life

A study was once conducted on people over the age of seventy that asked the question, "Once someone reaches that last quarter of life, what factor or factors can best predict the likelihood of them continuing to live? What helps a 70-year-old turn 71 or an 84-year-old turn 85?" The study examined dietary patterns, alcohol consumption, smoking habits, exercise habits, and other physical factors. It also looked at psycho-social factors including marital status, connection to friends and family, volunteering, etc. None of these things proved statistically significant in predicting the likelihood of continued longevity for the study subjects. One factor alone was found which could predict their chances of making it to that next birthday. That factor? Curiosity.

Curiosity creates a powerful cascade of physiological responses in our body-mind including heightened levels of dopamine production. This is one of the "feel-good" chemistries in your body. It keeps the cells of your body in growth mode, stimulating learning and evolution. Like our cells, we have only two modes of being: we are either growing or defending. Those over seventy need to keep that growth mode active or they can easily slip over the balance edge toward the dying side of life. Curiosity about both the outside and inside worlds is the key.

Unfortunately, curiosity is not something with which we are entirely comfortable. I know plenty of parents of four-year-olds who are ex-hausted by "Why?" and "How?" questions. Our educational institutions also seem exhausted by the same questions. Their goal has become the graduation of students who can give the "right" answers on a test, rather than the cultivation of creative explorers and life-long learners. Because of these early influences, most of us are not in the habit of fostering or cultivating curiosity, yet the benefits of doing so extend far beyond the simple possibility of a longer stay in your current body-mind. The quali-ty of that stay can be greatly enhanced as well.

A huge part of the great value I got from my Somatics and Feld-enkrais classes was the curiosity training they gave me. In each class, the instructor asked a multitude of questions, asking me to notice the fine details of how my body was moving. Could I lift that shoulder, but not move my ribs? Did all the ribs move? Did some stay still? These were details I had never thought to pay attention to, but the result of giving them my curious attention was deep healing.

Curiosity is a very open and relaxed state of mind. It is not judgmental in any way. It is interested. It is wondering. It seeks to gather more information, but does not feel compelled to put that data to use through the workings of the rational mind. It takes it all in and files it away, allowing room for all the brains of the body to process what has been received. The results that come are, therefore, not decided on by the linear, rational mind. The results are a natural and unfolding response of the whole body-mind.

Somatics and Feldenkrais classes do not have a "right" or "wrong" component to any of the movements. There is no perfect form you are trying to achieve. There is no specific goal to be achieved through the process of the class. There is only an experience of where you are right now in present time, and that experience is right and fine and perfect as it is. You are only asked to be present, to notice and have that experience. This is the pureness of curiosity.

Reframing a Story is the Power to Re-Create

When bacteria want to share important new information with one another, they swap genes. When we want to share important new information with one another, we swap stories. All cultures have their chosen stories. Stories are what create culture, because they carry the rules or guidelines of relationship with self, other, and world that people are expected to follow. Families have their chosen stories as well. These are the beliefs that we absorb as downloads while we are children. All of these stories give us a starting point for our life experience, but they are waiting for us to change them. Life seeks to evolve, and growing our stories is as important a part of that evolution as is the changing of our DNA.

We have seen how matter is created when curious awareness interacts with pure energy. It is as though our awareness is creating a framework, and energy uses that frame to become a solid particle. Stories work in the same way. They create a framework that patterns our awareness, creating the experiences of our lives. These story frameworks are the equivalent of computer software. They dictate how we will perceive and respond to our life's events, sometimes even at the level of our DNA. A well-timed and powerfully delivered story can turn a sugar pill and a glass of water into powerful healing agents capable of altering brain function or of eliminating cancer. The story delivered with a placebo creates the framework through which healing can happen. That framework is the blueprint for the relationship of the body to the substance it is about to ingest.

When Trinity died, I was stuck in a story framework that said, "Reincarnation is a linear process, happening one body at a time." With that frame in place, I could not accept that a 7-week-old puppy was my dog returning to me quickly and easily. When I dreamed about the Bishop's Lemon, I learned a new story about reincarnation, one that gave it a very different frame. I did not immediately believe that new story, but I opened up with pure curiosity to a new possibility. That opening was enough to create a happy ending.

When it comes to re-imagining, changing, or reframing the stories that are the software of these body-mind systems, curiosity is your best friend. Reframing your stories is not about positive thinking. It is not creating affirmations. It is not pretending you believe in things that you do not believe in. Reframing your stories is a dynamic engagement with curiosity and wonder. It is about remembering how to be a little child.

Would you like to create new results in any area of your life? Becoming aware of the stories you tell about that topic, and the framework you are providing for your perceptions is the most certain road to creating change in your life. Change your story framework, and you will have changed the blueprint for the set of relationships that create that area of your life. It may not be easy, but it is simple, and it does work.

Playtime! Cultivating Curiosity

For this exercise, I suggest going to a park or somewhere outdoors that contains both nature and people. I am going to ask you to observe yourself as well as things around you. This is a deceptively simple exercise, so remember to treat yourself with loving kindness before, during, and after this practice. Make sure you eat well beforehand, including some high-quality protein. Plan to fit in a short nap after your exercise, if at all possible.

Begin as always by getting comfortable. Choose a place to sit where your body feels relaxed and where you can easily observe your environment. Notice your breathing for two or three rounds. Give your attention to the feeling of the air flowing in and out, then spend a few minutes connecting to your senses. Notice all of the sounds you hear. Sniff the air and notice the smells. What flavors inhabit your tongue? What sensations do you feel on your skin?

Now, look around you with a soft, unfocused gaze, and let your attention stop with whatever seems to grab it. This may be a person; it may be a plant; it might be an animal or insect; it might be an empty park bench. Whatever the thing is, notice it. Look at the details of color, shape, and gesture. How is that person holding his shoulders? Are they rolled forward or pulled backward? Is that tree well-balanced or leaning to one side? Is there any damage on that bench – or tree, or person? Is the animal you are watching full of energy or more lethargic? These are examples of the kinds of details to look for.

Can you guess anything about the history of this thing based on your observations? Is your mind already telling you a story about this person, plant, animal, or object? If so, notice that story developing. Then, let it go.

Return your attention to your breathing, and notice your heart beating. Take a deep breath. Or three. With your attention still within, ask yourself, is there another way to see this? Let that question drop into your heart-field, take another breath, and gently return your attention to whatever you were observing. Does it appear any different to you? Does it feel any different to you? Notice whatever you are noticing now.

Take another breath and stretch and relax. Whether you noticed anything different or not is unimportant. The idea here is to become aware of your mind's inner workings, and to begin to develop a new habit, and that is the habit of connecting to your heart-field while asking yourself, *is there another way to see this?* This is a question that helps to keep curiosity active and your mind open to new thoughts, new ideas, and new story possibilities. This is a question that builds new roots and can rock your world. Try it often.

Seven

Food Circulates Love and Connection

Nowhere does our cultural confusion about the relationship of life and death affect us more than it does with food, because unless you happen to be a breatharian, in order for you to eat, something must die. I suppose that sounds rather callous, but it is a truth. A carrot plucked from the ground may not die in the same way that a cow does when taken to the abattoir, but it does not survive the processes of cooking or digestion any better. Eating is a gruesome business, or so it seems when we use the story frame called "life vs death" or "me, separate from everything outside my skin."

I think this basic confusion is why the list of foods that cause health problems or can kill us seems to be rapidly expanding. Red meat, bacon, and butter have been vilified for decades. Ancient staples such as wheat are now coming under fire as well. There seems to be an endless proliferation of new diets to cure us of the troubles caused by our food, with the basics of omnivorous or vegetarian now being joined by vegan, paleo, gluten-free, and raw – to name but a few. Even as supermarkets make it possible to eat anything we want from anywhere in the world at every season of the year, our ability to gain nourishment from that food seems to be diminishing.

Our relationship to food has changed dramatically over the past 100 years. Before the advent of supermarkets in the 20th century, the vast majority of people had a direct connection with the source of some, if not all, of their food. It was common to have known the pig or the cow that now sat on your table as a roast. It was common to have worked the soil that provided the carrots and potatoes accompanying your roast. It was common to have had a close relationship with the plants, animals, and soil that sustained you.

Most Americans no longer have any relationship with the source of their food. Supermarkets are not the source of food. They merely distribute it. Farmers are closer to the source, but are not the source itself. Farmers are facilitators. They create the conditions for food to grow, but without soil, water, sunlight, and the plants or animals that are our food, farmers would come up empty-handed. You eat soil, water, and sunlight through the transformational mediation of plants and animals who are assisted by bacterial and fungal allies. This is what food is. The source of food is not even a farm. The source of food is an ecosystem, or even a planet and solar system, a web of relationships that gathers and modifies energy and molecules into complex and nourishing substances. Creating a relationship with that source is a key part of receiving its nourishment, and I think soil is the best place to start.

Soil is Alive

When I use the word *soil* what pictures and associations come to your mind? Do you see a solid, brown substance in your mind's eye? Do you imagine plunging your hands into a dark and sweet-smelling garden bed? Do you remember getting yelled at as a kid for getting a party dress or a pair of good pants dirty? Do you think of that outstanding cabbage you made sauerkraut with that one year? Does anything come to mind?

I suspect that soil is not a regular topic of dinnertime conversation for most people living in modern America. It is something mostly taken for granted as that dirt beneath our feet – or beneath the concrete anyway. It grows the grass of our lawns, gets moved around to make way for new construction, and generally seems to be the one thing of which there is always plenty. The nightly news might occasionally remind us of the ever present problem of erosion of our topsoil, update us as to how much of that is being lost in the grain basket of the Midwest, and show us what is being done about it, but my sense is that soil is a dead topic for most people.

In my household, things are very different. We talk about soil on a daily basis, not because we have to, but because we love to. In the same way that some people wax eloquent over fine wines or fine cheeses, my husband and I enjoy all the subtleties of a good soil. What were the colors and textures that we had the privilege of working with that day? What do we need to do to help it along? How did it feel in our hands? What did it smell like?

The clay, sand, and silt that school textbooks emphasize as the main components of soil are like the flour in a cake. You need flour to make a cake (at least a traditional one), but flour is not cake. You need ground-up or broken-down rock to make soil, but until you add the other necessary ingredients, you've got what I think of as dirt. Living, healthy soil is more like cake, than it is like flour. It is springy and spongy and sweet. Unlike cake, there is nothing harmful about it. It is the place where the roots of health grow.

Creating living soil does not take oodles of hours spent digging and forking. It does not take a degree in biology or the ability to read a chemical analysis. Most of what you will need is carbon. Carbon is all the brown stuff that was once alive - like fallen leaves, straw, sawdust, and wood chips. Other organic matter in the form of green materials are fine: grass clippings or freshly plucked weeds, for example. They contain carbon as well as nitrogen and other beneficial nutrients. Animal manures are processed carbon, and there are many shades and variations here. Horses are relatively inefficient eaters, eliminating a lot of partly-digested organic matter. Cow manure is well-digested and rich in microbes. None of these things needs to be made into a compost pile (though, of course, that is good stuff too). Pile any greens or manure you have acquired on a chosen spot of plain dirt, top with the same amount or more of your brown carbon materials, making the whole thing twelve to eighteen inches deep, and step back and relax. If there is no rain in the forecast, then water your garden bed-to-be enough to wet it through, and you are done.

What you have just done is invited the third main component of soil to come and work in your garden bed. That third component is all the living stuff. It may be the earwigs and slugs who show up first. (I know, these are supposed to be bad, but they are actually useful decomposers.) It may be red wigglers or earthworms. Smaller creatures will also be making their appearances, the nematodes and springtails, perhaps. Bacteria and fungi are already present and will be growing substantially in numbers. These are the key players whose ability to secrete the chemicals needed to digest cellulose make the whole thing work. If you were to do nothing else for your pile of carbon and organic matter, then depending on temperatures and rainfall, you will have the beginnings of a fine, living soil in a few months to a year.

I say beginnings because as with fine wine or hard cheeses, it takes some time to make great soil. Nature uses centuries or even millennia to do it. With regular additions of organic matter to your new bed, you can do it over the course of a few years to a decade.

Unfortunately, the kind of soil I am talking about here is no longer common in agriculture. It isn't all that common in gardens either. About a half-century ago, our thinking about soil took a sharp turn into chemistry, leaving the biology out. We have spent billions of dollars and decades of energy trying to manipulate the chemistry of the soil to grow more and more plants for food. What we are discovering is that this is a treadmill, a race we can never win. A soil of clay or sand or silt that is devoid of life is no more capable of growing healthy and nutritious plants than is a bowl of flour that is devoid of fats and sugar and leavening agents capable of making a great cake. You need all the ingredients, and for soil that especially includes biology and organic matter.

Biology Manipulates Chemistry

Biology is the biggest anomaly in all of modern science. Accounting for the existence of living things is a hard task in a universe that is supposed to have unfolded randomly and accidentally. Statistically, we seem to be very lucky that the early molecules of our planet formed any amino acids at all, much less the 22 needed for the building of our bodies.

Understanding the transformative role of living things in a mechanistic and accidental universe is not actually possible, because living organisms defy all odds. In purely mechanistic systems, everything is moving toward entropy. Just as your car will one day break down and be incapable of repairing itself, so too would a mechanical universe eventually break down and be beyond repair. Living things do just the opposite. They not only repair themselves, they learn and grow and become more complex over time. They evolve, and Gaia has certainly proved her ability to evolve.

This same evolution happens in soil that is filled with living organisms. Living organisms confer on dirt the ability to repair itself by capturing water and the other atoms and molecules that are essential to the health and well-being of the creatures of the land. Living things turn dirt into soil; soil that becomes much more complex over time. When the first bacteria crawled onto bare rock, there was no soil. Now there are millions of species and varieties of bacteria, as well as an amazing variety of soils capable of supporting a huge diversity of plant and animal communities. The two go hand-in-hand.

When we discovered chemistry, we thought we had found something that superseded biology. We thought we had found the building blocks of biological systems, the *things* that controlled and explained the behaviors of bacteria, fungi, cells – and ultimately ourselves. It turns out, however, that biology at every scale of life is manipulating chemistry. We have seen what amazing chemists the plants are. Bacteria and fungi, the primary builders of our soils, are no less skilled at the manipulation of atoms and molecules. They use their own bodies as the factories in which compounds are made which can break down cellulose or build water-catching networks of humus. They create serotonins, the same neurotransmitter used in our brains. All bodies can be influenced by chemicals, but all bodies also have elaborate systems designed to regulate how those chemicals influence us. Chemistry is one of the tools available to all biological organisms. Biology uses chemistry to create its environment, whether we are talking about plants, animals, bacteria, or people.

When we treat the planet's soils like dirt, like an inert and dead substance that operates through a set of mechanistic chemical interactions, then we are missing as much as 80% of what is happening in a living soil. A huge percentage of healthy soil is made up of living organisms and the results of their activities; this includes the roots of plants, the dead bodies of once-living organisms, the exudates of all these living organisms, and humus – a still mysterious, carbon-based molecular chain that confers balance and stability to living soils. It is the interactions of all these organic parts that allows nutrients to be both stored and available as food when needed. Bacteria and fungi are the members of this system that extract nutrients from rock particles and dead plant materials. They hold these nutrients in their bodies until they are eaten by nematodes or protozoa, or until they trade them directly to a plant root. As bacteria and fungi are eaten, the nutrients they contain that are not needed by the nematodes or protozoa are excreted, becoming available to the plants. This is the beginning of the soil food web, a complex and rich process of interlocking relationships that creates a healthy soil ecosystem.

Soil is like a multicellular organism in many ways. The broken-down rock that forms its skeletal structure requires the work of trillions of diverse creatures to create a body. Those creatures perform all the functions of our body organs, including respiration, circulation, filtering, and information exchange. As happens in our bodies when we use drugs to improve our body functions, using chemicals in soil can create unforeseen "side-effects." Many of these side-effects happen because they kill or maim the soil's microbiota, eliminating the complex relationships of the soil food web. When we use chemical fertilizers, nutrients that were once held in the soil by its creatures are instead leached out by rainfall or irrigation, leaving the soil poorer while causing many downstream difficulties.

Soil, like all things, is created through relationships, and these relationships work together to build a networked system that is in turn a foundation for more diversity of things and more relationships between them. Eating is an important and large part of these foundational relationships because eating keeps energy and molecules circulating. Our insistence on seeing eating as a win-lose, competitive relationship has blinded us to some of its deeper possibilities, and to its essential role in creating and evolving living organisms. When we garden and farm in ways that enhance all of the complex relationships that create soil rather than destroy those relationships, we create a sound root system for our own health and well-being, a root system that can be created in no other way. We create food that connects us to the One life that surrounds and supports us.

What is in our Food?

Plants thriving in living, microbial-rich soil are not the same as plants eking out an existence in a barren dirt substrate. The calories contained in such plants may be the same, but the nutrient density is not. Nutrient studies of plants conducted over the past century show a consistent downward trend in the amount of minerals contained in our plant and animal foods. Levels of everything from calcium to zinc are consistently less than they were in the foods eaten by our grandparents and great-grandparents. There are other factors too - a whole host of phytochemicals, molecules created by plants and their microbial allies that provide antioxidant and other benefits to our bodies – that were not being measured a century ago. We have no idea how these have changed under the increasing pressure of a chemically-oriented agriculture.

Agricultural practices that consider only the chemical components of soil have lost the store of minerals from our soils because they have killed the microbial populations that held them in place. Water passing through a dirt substrate leaches out minerals and nutrients, sending them back to the sea in toxic overloads that kill the microbiota of river deltas and the larger network of fish and animal communities that inhabit these regions. In these monocultural, chemically-manipulated agricultural systems, no one wins or thrives, including us.

There is even more to food than calories, nutrients, and phytochemicals. There are subtler energetics, reflections of the web of relationship (or lack of it) that cradled this food as it grew, and that we still find hard to measure. Lack of a technology that can measure does not mean these factors do not exist, however. We know that we live steeped in the subtle electromagnetics of nature's nervous system, and that our hearts and bodies are sensitive to these subtle energies. We also know that we live in a quantum-based universe, one that is created through the interaction of awareness and energy. As plants and animals grow, they too are steeped in these electromagnetic and quantum energy fields and their bodies are filled with the information gleaned from this immersion. When we eat, we are absorbing this subtle information from our food, as well as the more measurable calories and nutrients.

There is a Chinese proverb that tells us that the most valuable fertilizer is a farmer's footprints. On the surface, this can be translated as meaning that the time a farmer spends walking her farm and observing the animals, plants, and soil is the key to creating a healthy and productive farm. The farmer will notice what needs to be done with good timing. He will notice all the little things, like the aphids starting to gather on the wormwood, and will be able to learn from the farm itself where its strengths and weaknesses lie. Time spent walking a farm or garden is an important part of growing healthy plants and living soils, but I believe there is a more literal meaning to this proverb as well.

A farmer is an electromagnetic oscillator whose presence and attention has a direct influence on the living components of the farm. The animals, plants, insects, and soils of a farm are all in relationship with the farmer. They respond to the words, thoughts, and feelings of the farmer – just as houseplants have been shown to respond to their care-givers. A plant in a rich, personal, and intimate relationship with a farmer will convey a very different vibration - a very different infor-mation frequency - when it becomes food, than that conveyed by a plant that watched a tractor with a sealed and air-conditioned cab pass through its field. Humans are part of nature, and our attention and awareness and curiosity are required for good health to spread through the natural sys-tems with which we interact.

For many years I heard a common refrain from many of my landscap-ing clients. In one way or another they would say to me, "The garden seems different after you've been here. Everything seems better." I as-sumed this meant they liked my style of designing, planting, weeding, and mulching – and yet I knew that wasn't what they were talking about. Then one day I walked with some trepidation into a private session with a well-respected channeler to talk with a being known as Alcazar. Over the course of our session, Alcazar encouraged me to become aware of how much my consciousness was influencing the soils that I worked with. He encouraged me to take off my gloves more often and run my hands through the soil, not needing to know what I was doing, simply aware that benefit was being created in that process. The electromagnetic oscillations of the human body-mind are powerful indeed, rippling through all that we contact and entering our food.

Linking Our Microbiome to the Soil Microbiome

The discovery of the role of bacteria in collaborating with our cells to create these human bodies is a revolutionary medical discovery. Doctors and medical researchers are equating it with the discovery of a new or-gan, one that is vital to every aspect of our health and well-being. A similar discovery has been unfolding in soil sciences over the past few decades as researchers have discovered the essential relationships that plant roots develop with fungi and bacteria in the soil. Just as we rely on bacteria to educate and inform our immune systems, so too do plants. Just as we rely on the DNA of bacteria to code some of the proteins used in our bodies, so too do plants. Just as we rely on our gut flora to digest and make available to us some of the nutrients in the foods we ingest, so too do plants rely on bacteria and fungi to find and make available some of the nutrients essential to plant growth and health. Just as human mothers make HMOs to feed their babies' microbes, so too do plants make and exude through their roots a wide range of carbohydrates that are specifically for the microbes in the soil.

The first strand in the web of health for all multicellular organisms is a relationship with a diverse array of the microbes that co-evolved with and within us. Humans, plants, animals, even insects – all of us rely on our microbes, our personal microbiome, to keep us healthy. Each individual microbiome does not exist in isolation, however, from the wider microbiota of soil and plants and animals, any more than our bodies exist separate from the world around us. Our personal microbiota need their own connection to the wider world in order for them to stay balanced and healthy. The increasing incidence of auto-immune diseases including asthma and irritable bowel syndrome is now being tied to our hyper-sanitation practices and overuse of antibiotics. It turns out that our immune systems need a regular workout or they go bonkers on us. That regular workout happens when we are regularly exposed – inside and out – to the microbes of the world around us, and especially to those in living soil.

As a gardener of living soils, I am in continual connection with a vibrant microbial world. I often handle horse, cow, or goat manure during the course of a day in addition to the sweet, dark-brown soils that I love to crumble between my fingers. I also rarely wash my hands, perhaps two or three times a day on average. Lunch is almost always eaten with dirty hands, a practice that many of you may be shuddering at as you read this, but my immune system seems to love me for it. My gut microbes have daily and lengthy conversations with their brethren in the outside world, most of whom are likely just passing through without staying for a long visit. Over the past ten years, I have averaged less than one episode of a cold or a flu per year, and nothing more serious than that.

Whether you are a fan of Facebook or a reader of a daily paper, reflect on how different your life would be if you had no access to these hits of daily news. How isolated would you feel? Would your ability to make decisions be affected? Take away a chance for gossip with friends as well, and you would be living a very different life from what you currently know. Our focus on super-cleanliness and ultra-sanitation has created a similar situation for the bacteria and other beneficial microbes that inhabit our guts. Without connection to the organisms of a living soil, they find themselves adrift in a world that is difficult to understand and prepare for. The current slew of probiotics hitting the marketplace can help to put beneficial microbes into your gut that may be missing, but those microbes will still need regular connection to the outside world to perform at their best.

There is certainly a need for some sanitation practices. Operating rooms immediately come to mind, as does washing hands after going to the restroom or handling toxic chemicals. There is no question that antibiotics have saved quite a few lives, though it is also becoming clear that our regular use of them is causing a host of chronic health problems – including obesity. They may also be a contributing factor in autism and dementia because our brains rely heavily on our gut microbes in order to function well. We need our trillion cells working alongside a diversity of collaborative bacteria if we are to experience optimal health.

Diversity is an important marker for healthy and resilient ecosystems, and this is no less true for our internal microbiome. As researchers now explore the microbial communities in our colons, they find that Americans consistently have the least internal microbial diversity, especially when compared to Africans. This lack of diversity does not stop within the human population of the United States, however. Jonathan Lundgren, a researcher with the USDA, has found low diversity of bacteria in the stomachs of insects living in our monoculture agricultural systems as compared to those eating in fields with a diversity of plant life. Each piece of this puzzle, this web of nature, harbors its own community of microbes. Limiting our exposure to these other communities, failing to embrace a wider diversity in our food choices as well as failing to foster a wider diversity of microbes through the cultivation of living soils, is a choice that is limiting our health and our future possibilities.

Food is intimate, and discussion of our food choices can quickly become a highly-charged topic. I remember running screaming from the kitchen as a ten-year-old on a Saturday morning because my mother wanted me to try some new and ugly-looking food called granola. She persevered in getting me to try just one bite. I discovered an unexpected sweetness and a crunchiness that felt delightful, and I ate that bowl of granola. I have found, however, that I am not alone in having strong opinions about food and what I will and won't try. Inhaling the aromas of whatever lies on your plate, tasting its flavors, feeling its texture with your tongue, this is an experience that is highly personal and partly erotic. This thing called food is about to join with you, to become you. Especially when the relationship is new, caution and deliberation may be advised, but not at the expense of your learning and growth – or your health.

Food is the great connector, and I no longer see eating as a process of winning and losing or competing and surviving. I see eating as a part of my conversation with and immersion in the natural world. As I eat, I take in molecules that buzz with information as well as with nutrition. As I eat, my body learns about the world I live in - in ways I can barely imagine. As I eat, I am offered the possibility of becoming like that which I eat. As I eat, I participate in the continuum of being that creates this one life of which I am blessed to be a part.

A Lesson in Love from Miss Cow

I have mentioned that I had my years as a vegetarian and discovered that the vegetarian diet did not bring me excellent health. When I returned to meat eating, I found better choices available in grocery stores than I had 15 years previous, but I still wasn't thrilled with the way animals were being raised, so I learned to butcher my own chickens. I also bought a share in a cow.

My husband and I had recently bought our homestead and were in the early stages of its evolution when together with some friends, we bought a 3-month-old Hereford calf. We named her Miss Cow as a defense against getting too attached to what would eventually be an 18-month-old heifer that we would butcher. She started out living with our friends, but eventually came to live on our place.

Miss Cow had spent her first 3 months living on a ranch, roaming large pastures with her mother and the others in her herd. She was not comfortable with human beings, preferring to keep us at a distance as much as possible. Fortunately, our group of friends had also purchased a young Jersey calf at about the same time. This second calf, Brownie, was to become our dairy cow someday. She and Miss Cow provided companionship for each other while they grew up, and, as the product of a dairy, Brownie also demonstrated to Miss Cow that humans weren't all that scary.

My husband is the animal person in our family. He has a great love for all animals as well as a knack for working with them. In the case of Miss Cow, he spent months slowly acclimating her to human touch and handling. He would supplement the pasture that she and Brownie were on with alfalfa hay, bringing them a flake each day. As they came to eat, he would stand beside Brownie, but reach over her to rub Miss Cow's back and shoulders. He taught Miss Cow to accept a halter, making it easier to lead the cows to different pastures and possible to load them into a trailer. Miss Cow was not easy to lead, but would go wherever we led Brownie.

As Miss Cow grew, she became a gentler animal. She liked having her shoulders rubbed and was comfortable eating while I picked up the manure in the corral that she shared with Brownie in her final winter. In spite of what was coming, I fell in love with her. I have found that cows, in general, are calm and soothing creatures to be around. Standing near a cow who is happily munching grass or chewing her cud is akin to sitting with an old tree. It is soothing to my human nervous system. I loved being around Miss Cow. I started to think about keeping her.

The time came, however, when our friends were ready to fill their freezer. My husband and I could think of no way to buy them out and substitute for her meat, and so we made a date with a "kill guy," someone willing to kill your animal for you and who also comes with a truck equipped to hoist a 1,000 pound carcass off the ground and prep it for hanging.

In the week before Miss Cow's death, we did two things. First, we created a special pen for the slaughter to take place, then practiced leading Brownie and Miss Cow to it each day. We wanted the experience to be as stress-free as possible for Miss Cow – just another day walking to the pen for some food. We needed Brownie to lead her there, but would return Brownie alone to the corral before the slaughter.

Second, we prepared for and held a ceremony of thanksgiving. The ceremony was held the day before the kill. Several friends joined us, and my husband and I talked about the joy we felt in raising Miss Cow, the many gifts she had already given us through her presence, and our gratefulness for the nourishment that her body would provide to us. We smudged ourselves with sage, and asked for an easy death for Miss Cow and for her awareness of our appreciation. I left the ceremony feeling blessed and tremendously grateful.

We were haltering Miss Cow and Brownie by 6:30 the next morning. Miss Cow was calm, but Brownie was less so. My husband led Brownie from the corral. I followed with Miss Cow. Brownie was giving my husband some trouble, not walking easily, but Miss Cow stepped right past her, pulling me with her as she headed directly to the pen. I shut the gate behind her. My husband turned and led Brownie back to the corral. It was the first time Miss Cow had ever gone anywhere without Brownie. I sat beside her while she ate her hay, saying *thank you* and looking in her eyes. She looked back at me with calmness, with acceptance - and with something more. In all my life, I have rarely felt so loved. It was hard to take in that much love.

I know now that all eating has the potential to be a communion. We take in that which we wish to be. In this case, I was preparing to take in great strength, calmness, and love. Love is a word that can be hard to define or understand. From Miss Cow, it was not a word, it was an experience. She was preparing to become me by feeding me, and she did not regret the opportunity.

Her last day as Miss Cow went smoothly. Her death was quick, and every part of her, including her hide, went to someone who would use it. It was an emotional day for me, as I allowed myself to take in for the first time the enormity of what it means to eat. Eating means I am not separate or alone. Eating makes me one with the body of Nature – or Life or God, or whatever you wish to call it. Eating connects me to the circulation of an energy that is hinted at in the word, *love*. Eating can do this for all of us.

Playtime! Connect to Soil

Several years ago I saw a posting on Facebook showing a picture of a cluster of people gathered at a climate change demonstration. A man stood out in the crowd, boldly holding up a sign that read, "Gardens and Curiosity Will Save the World." I couldn't agree more.

The aware use of your curiosity, which I hope this book is awakening, is a critical part of making the changes we need to make if we are to live sustainably – or better regeneratively – on this wondrous planet. Using that aware curiosity to grow a garden that will provide some of your food will complete a circuit, to use an electrical metaphor, that is critical to a full understanding of what it means to be a part of this living Earth.

A complete course in holistic gardening will have to wait for another book, but in this one I want to suggest that you start by becoming a soil-connoisseur and a soil-lover. Soil is the foundation of our health, both as individuals and collectively as a civilization. Our currently divisive economic and political systems reflect the barren and distraught condition of our soils, and vice versa. Change the soil that feeds you, and you might be surprised at how that change works its way through every system and relationship in your life.

A good place to begin is by following the simple instructions outlined earlier to create a bed of living soil. If you have no access to a backyard of your own, perhaps you can borrow some space in someone else's. Guerrilla gardening in a surreptitious corner of an empty lot, a park, or some other public place is also possible. Your goal here is only to watch the process of growing living soil, and to create a place into which you can dip your hands on occasion.

Make a small pile of all the dried and green materials you have found. Green ones go beneath, brown ones on top. Three feet long by three feet wide and eighteen inches tall is a good minimum size, but the dimensions can vary according to the space, your needs, and available materials. Water is a crucial element to activate the biology. For quickest results, keep the pile moist on the inside, but not sopping wet. You will have to stick a hand in occasionally to check the moisture level of the pile.

While this deep mulch pile is decomposing and growing into soil, begin to make it a regular practice to meet the soils in your area. Is there a wild place near you, perhaps a forested area in a park or near a river? Visit this place and spend some time digging into its soils. Bring a small trowel with you, and try to find a spot that has a cover of leaves left intact on it. Carefully put these to the side, and examine the layer beneath. Are there half decomposed bits of leaves here? What is the texture of this layer? The smell? Do some more digging, noticing each layer as you go. How does the color change? Do you see living creatures? Which ones? Does the texture change? Is it gritty or silky? How moist is each layer?

I suggest continuing until it becomes difficult to dig with a trowel. How deep were you able to go? When you are done, return the soil to the hole and put the leafy layer back on top.

Follow a similar process in other places in this same wild area and in your own backyard. Soils can be remarkably different just a few feet apart. Look at the soils in your friends' yards and in front of the public library. Begin to see for yourself what the soils around you are like, and return regularly to check on the progress of your mulch pile. At your next meal, take a moment to wonder, *what was the texture and smell of the soil that grew this food? Was it a living soil?*

Eight

You are an Intelligent Cell in the Gaian Body

After 4 billion years of learning and evolution, Earth has become an intricately networked system of self-organizing and self-repairing parts, akin to the organs, cells, and microbes of our bodies. Some of Earth's organs are as massive as the atmosphere, the oceans, and the continents. Some of her microbes are as small as a virus. Within the bounded-infinity of our planetary system, the diversity of all of these organisms is beyond our current ability to count and record.

There are known to be over 10,000 species of bacteria, with many biologists estimating the true number of distinct species to be in the millions. There are at least 350,000 species of beetles living around the planet, though again the full number of species is estimated to be in the millions. Trees are estimated to be at minimum 10,000 species with some estimates in the 100,000 range. (Isn't it rather amazing that we don't have a more exact number for trees? How much do we really know about this place that is our home? Or is it simply more fluid than we currently like to imagine?) This diversity is a part of Gaia's fractal nature. It is part of the non-linear, infinite process that is her life.

Once Life invented duality, two-ness, there was no reason to stop the process of individuation. A tricycle balances more easily than a bicycle, and a four-wheeler does it even easier. Systems with built-in back-ups are more resilient than systems with no back-up at all. The diversity of relationships created by this huge diversity of microbes, cells, and organisms is what gives us the illusion of stability all around, cloaking the essential and dynamic, always changing and adjusting flows of information, energy, and materials that surround and move through us. This sense of consistency and stability is why we so often forget that our bodies are much like rivers, constantly changing even as they appear the same.

A garden is, once again, the setting that taught me to appreciate and cultivate diversity. A row of cabbages or corn plants, all lined up like soldiers in formation, are more like sitting ducks than they are like a battalion. They are easy prey, with no cover or camouflage from predators, whether those predators are large, like deer, or small, like moths. The lack of diversity above ground is also reflected in a lack of diversity below ground, especially if the soil is nakedly exposed to the sun and rain. There will be food and housing for only a few species of microbes, most likely a few bacteria, with little or no fungi present. This means the roots will be working very hard to provide for themselves, without the benefit of a strong team of allies to support their growth and development.

Contrast this picture with that of a garden allowed to grow more wildly – more in keeping with nature's collaborative balancing. Like Gabe Brown's mix of cover crops, it may seem riotous and chaotic, but it will be more stable and healthier. My gardens now pair cabbages with onions and cilantro and parsley. The ground is covered with mulch when things are small, keeping the soil from developing a crust to protect itself from heat and rain, because such a crust will also inhibit its respiration. (Yes, soil breathes. That is part of being alive.) Weeds will germinate and join my own plantings, and I will welcome many of them to add to the blending of species.

Dandelion and chicory with their deep tap roots are always appreciated, as they forage for minerals and bring them to the surface. These are also good food for me, adding to my own vibrant health as well as the soil's. Mallow and vetches may show up, or the seeds dropped by last year's planting of Malabar spinach may add to the mix. Members of the grass family will invariably want to join the party as well. Their fibrous roots can work wonders in breaking up heavy clay soils. I may trim these off a few inches from the ground to encourage them to slough off some of those roots, adding valuable carbon to the soil. This carbon feeds the soil microbes. I fork my soils a little before planting, thus adding some oxygen to enhance the soil's respiration, but I do so without turning the soil. This ensures that I do not kill off the fungi and bacteria already present, leaving them free to quickly establish relationships with the mix of plants in this mini-ecosystem, offering their support as allies to the plants.

Connection and relationship are the critical elements behind nature's use of diversity. A garden – or a planet – of many unrelated parts is no more stable or vibrant than is a monoculture of soybeans. It is the relationships that make it all work, and nature is a master at forging relationships that are mutually beneficial. There is no win-lose game in nature. Infinity requires win-win. Four billion years of evolving diversity has been achieved through collaboration for a mutual goal, not competition for an immediate need. While it is fun to ask, "How many species of bacteria are there?" the real question is, "How many collaborative relationships does one bacterial species develop?" It is the diversity of beneficial relationships, as much as the diversity of things, that creates the stability we so love. The vast diversity of species on this small, round planet is a reflection of a partner-dance called collaboration, and this is a dance we too can learn.

The Opportunity in Problems

As we enter the era of Earth's sixth Great Extinction, it is the loss of species diversity and the destabilizing effect that has on Earth's finely-balanced webs of relationships that has scientists feeling so concerned and scared. Extinction events do, however, seem to be a part of evolution. In your own life, when have you done the most growing and evolving? Was it when everything was nice and comfy and stable? Or was it when life threw you a curve ball – and you missed the hit? I know for myself it was the broken arm, the boyfriends who didn't love me back, and other disappointments or challenges that made me grow into someone new.

For most of us it is the uncomfortable and destabilizing moments that cause the most growth and personal evolution. I once had a woman tell me that cancer was the best thing that ever happened to her because it taught her to take herself and life more lightly and to be happy here and now. I wouldn't be writing this book right now if my life had not been destabilized the day my husband shattered his tibia.

There are grave dangers in these moments of destabilization. The cancer patient might have died too quickly to get the blessing of happiness. My husband's injury could have thrown us into financial panic and loss. Yet, clearly, these destabilizations are also moments of tremendous potential and immense possibility. This is where Earth stands now. She has been destabilized. The old diversity is no longer intact, and it is too late to go back and reestablish it. We can't undo centuries of abuse and neglect any more than my husband could un-jump from the ditch that shattered his tibia or the cancer patient could undo the causes of her cancer.

Forward is our only direction. The best questions are not how to maintain an old and teetering stability, but how to collaborate with Earth and nature in creating the new relationships that will foster a new balance and a new stability that is even more glorious and beautiful than the one into which we were born. The previous five Great Extinctions on this planet led to five Great Blossomings, times when the diversity and complexity of species and ecosystems made great leaps that would have been hard to predict based on what came before. A sixth Great Blossoming is not only possible, it is likely.

The first Great Extinction was caused by the evolution on this planet of photosynthesis. Oxygen, a highly flammable gas, is a byproduct of photosynthesis. It took millions of years from the time the first cyano-bacteria evolved and began breathing out oxygen, but eventually oxygen began to build in the atmosphere to levels that caused spontaneous combustion. Imagine being a microscopic algae, floating on the surface of an ancient ocean, when suddenly the air above you is on fire. Whoops! The threat to the survival of Earth's nascent species was real. It probably took a few millennia, but the inventive microbes who are our ancestors responded with the evolution of bacteria who utilized oxygen, breathing it in and carbon dioxide out. Our atmosphere is now a delicately-balanced array of gases, with oxygen maintained at levels high enough to support the oxygen-breathers, but not so high as to be spontaneously combustible.

The first Great Extinction was an inside job, and that humans may be the cause of the sixth Great Extinction is, therefore, not without precedent. The response of the planet's microbes to that first extinction may also be a guide for us in responding to this sixth. The first Great Extinction was caused by a lack of balance, and I believe the same is true of this sixth one. Human beings are part of nature. We are an intricately designed and complex creature. I do not believe the balance now required will be fulfilled by the evolution of some second creature to balance our actions. The balance required will come from within us.

For millennia, humans have been creating cultural systems that emphasize the rational and linear approach of the left hemisphere of our head-brain. We have downplayed the role and abilities of the right hemisphere brain and shut down the brain functions of the heart and gut to the best of our ability. These are the systems within us that perform the critical balancing function needed by our left brain. These are the systems that make us a balanced and fully-functioning species. These are the abilities we will redevelop as we walk the path to a symbiotic, mutually-beneficial and loving relationship with our planet.

The development of a highly active left brain is likely an important part of our evolution as a species. The abilities this part of our body-mind system provides are useful, to say the least. They are not our only abilities, however, and they are not as useful solo as they are with the whole package of the body-mind. A computer that can read and write and process around 40 bits of information per second is great. Hook that computer up to one that works in parallel and processes millions of bits of information per second, and you have a machine with real capabilities. This is the internal shift we can choose to make.

Cultivating Connection and Communication

As we learn to develop balance within our whole body-mind, we will naturally rediscover our abilities for interspecies communication and for connection with all the parts of this living Earth. This connection with the larger world is an essential part of the path to a sixth Great Blossoming. We cannot solve the ecological problems we have created on our own – precisely because it is our isolation that has created them. Anna Breytenbach is a skilled animal communicator from South Africa who describes humans as suffering from "separation sickness." We have forgotten our inherent oneness with all the other living parts of this planet. We have forgotten that we are all in this together, creatively and collaboratively.

Anna has demonstrated an impressive facility in communicating with and understanding animals, including potentially dangerous animals such as leopards and baboons. In a fascinating video about her work, she repeatedly reported verifiable information that was unknown to her through any other channel than that of talking to the animal in question. Whether it is the attachment of a parakeet to its former owner or the concern of a leopard for two unrelated cubs from which it has been separated, Anna's ability to connect with the animals around her brings change and healing to all concerned. This is a capacity that lies latent in all humans, but requires our willingness and commitment to reawaken. (See Resources for a link to the video about Anna.)

Animals are not the only intelligent creatures on this planet, and not the only ones we can communicate with. Plant communicators are also appearing in Western culture helping us to learn to recognize and respect the wisdom of this kingdom of beings as well. Specialists in insect and microbe communication are sure to come, and are probably already present among our children. All of these kingdoms will provide us with the links needed to connect to the holistic intelligence of Earth herself.

Can you imagine what a conversation with Gaia would feel like?

As a gardener, I have focused on cultivating the ability to communicate with plants, but this skill is not one that came naturally to me, at least not as an adult. I know this skill is natural to humans and is carried by our young children, but it is also one of the first abilities from which we train them away. Fortunately, relearning this kind of interspecies communication skill is both possible and infinitely rewarding.

I was in my teens when I first became aware that there were people living within Western cultures who could communicate with plants. Two of the founders of the Findhorn garden, Eileen Caddy and Dorothy Maclean, had such abilities. I devoured the books I could find about Findhorn, a seemingly magical garden growing in the sandy soils of Scotland that grew giant cabbages and other marvels of the plant world. I was not yet a gardener myself, but I loved the idea of being in such close communion with nature. However, my attempts to communicate with wild plants seemed to bring no results.

Almost a decade later, after I had become a gardener and food grower, I discovered the books of Machaelle Small Wright, creator of the Perelandra garden. Wright's style is different than that of the Findhorn gardeners. She makes extensive use of applied kinesiology, also called muscle testing, to link with and receive feedback from the nature spirits and plant devas. Deva is a term borrowed from Sanskrit meaning *the shining ones*. It is used to describe the soul consciousness of the plant kingdom. I spent one growing season carefully applying the Perelandra techniques in my own small backyard. By the end of that fall, I was ready to pull my hair out. The garden had done okay, but, again, I felt no increase in my connection to nature.

I moved on to books by Michael Roads, the *Talking with Nature* series. Here again I found someone who could connect with devas and nature spirits, but I still struggled to replicate his experiences or results. It took the passage of yet another decade before I would discover *The Secret Teachings of Plants*, by Stephen Harrod Buhner. It was this book that helped me to understand in a left brain, rational way what was needed for plant communication to become a reality for me. In spite of the title of Buhner's book, it is as much about the secrets of the human body, and especially our hearts, as it is about the secret teachings of plants.

Prior to reading Buhner's book, I had been looking for the equivalent of a lightning bolt. I was expecting the veils to part inside my mind, for my perceptions to open and reveal to me the forms of nature spirits and devas all around, as seemed to be the case for Roads, Wright, Caddy, and Maclean. What I learned to do instead was to believe in the reality of my body's subtle cues, to listen to the quiet whisper in my mind and not dismiss it out of hand as a figment of my imagination. I learned to make space for the possibility that my heart was in communication with my brain and that it did indeed have the power to communicate with the electromagnetic field of a plant.

I do not know if I am communicating with devas, nature spirits, or the plants themselves, but in my experience it feels as though I am conversing with an individual who has a collective standing right behind them, so that is how I think of and describe it. The wisdom I receive from these amazing beings is often surprising and unexpected. I find myself knowing things I didn't know I knew – because the pathway has come through my heart. This is one of the markers I now use to verify my plant communication experiences: was there an element of surprise? If so, and if it feels good, then I know I am in the zone or frequency of my heart-mind and am benefiting from true connection.

You are part of nature. Your connection to this planet is not severed, it is simply waiting for your renewed attention. Returning to connection with ***your*** heart's guidance will reconnect you to nature's intelligence, leading to the actions that are there for you to take to collaborate in the next planetary evolution. No one can know this for you. Your guidance is within.

Using the Living Body as Our Guide

For far too long, we have let the concept of *machine* guide our thinking about ourselves and this planet, building schools and farms that resemble factories – or even prisons. We have dreamed the nightmare of survival of the fittest in a dangerous world of life vs. death, creating economic systems that ignore or combat the environment, as well as legal and po-litical systems that work to accumulate decision-making power in the hands of a few. It is time to awaken from this nightmare and see the deeper reality that surrounds us: There is one life, and we are intimately and completely part of it.

As we learn to embrace this truth, we will begin to see around us the body of a living planet that offers us the opportunity to embrace our role as intelligent cells. We will learn to design our human systems in ways that support Gaia's evolution as well as our own. Farms will become mini-ecosystems, linked together to participate in the well-being of the larger ecosystems that host them. Education, learning, and play will be part of every era of our lives, not something reserved only for youth. Money will be designed to mimic blood flow through a healthy body, reaching every person in amounts that support their well-being, and we will find some other substance to mimic the fat cells that give our bodies a healthy storage reserve. Our legal system will embrace connection and communication and sharing of information, and our political system will work to foster collaborative diversity.

Both farmers and doctors will be first and foremost ecologists, con-cerned with the interactions and relationships happening in the soil of both the planet and our bodies. The inner garden of our guts will be seen as an extension of the outer garden of Gaia, and because of that farmers will be thought of as our first doctors, with health professionals and medical professionals being our back-up systems. As every profession learns to embrace the study of relationship, entanglement, and ecology, we will create a very different world.

Finding Our Way to That Different World

Europeans had developed the technologies needed to cross the Atlantic Ocean at least a hundred years before Columbus set sail. Technology was not the issue; beliefs and stories were. We currently have ample technologies for living sustainably on this planet. We have ample technologies for creating collaborative, synergistic systems that add to Earth's ecological diversity and evolution. What we have lacked are the beliefs, the story framework needed, to mobilize those technologies and put them to use in broad and comprehensive ways.

This book contains the young root, the radicle, of a story that can lead us into collaborative relationship with our planet: Curious awareness is a magic key that unlocks our creative healing and growing power, while showing us the long tradition of intelligent collaboration that has driven the evolution of life on Earth. With our wise heart-brains as guides, we can use our curiosity and our awareness to connect with Nature's nervous system, tapping into a reservoir of wisdom that knows of life's wholeness and of the fractal pathways that build diversity within that wholeness. We will eat from this intelligent planet's infinite and continuing creation, knowing that to do so connects us to more levels of her wisdom as well as to that circulating life energy that is hinted at in the word, *love*. As this life energy circulates in us, we will learn to participate more fully as conscious, collaborative creators, becoming intelligent cells in the Gaian body, which is part of the Solar body, and part of a living Universe.

By giving your attention and awareness to this story many times a day, you will enliven this young root, feeding its growth and evolution. You will be participating in the process of bringing this story to the top of search engine results, not on the internet, but in the human morphic field. It will get easier to tell this story – and to know it to be true. As this story grows its roots in you, the culture that these roots feed will become a physical reality.

I do believe that the evolution of humanity is a game-changer for this planet, on a par with the evolution of photosynthesis. The world we will inhabit as the sixth Great Extinction eventually gives way to the sixth Great Blossoming may not be predictable based on what we know now, but I am certain it will be both remarkable and beautiful. I say that because of something else Hawthorne taught me.

A week after my first journey with Hawthorne, I found myself at the end of a day of working in a client's garden. There were several hawthorne trees laden with large, red berries at the edge of the garden, and so when I had finished my work, I went up to the trees and asked for permission to pick their berries. Permission was granted, and I began to fill my basket.

I had been participating in a personal growth training program that asked me to answer the question, *Who am I?* I was giving this question some thought as I picked the berries, when I decided to ask the Hawthorne's opinion. I silently asked the tree, *Who do you know me to be?* The answer was immediate, visceral, and wholly without spoken language. I felt it in my gut first, a pulse of power and wisdom that travelled up to my brain. It felt so much bigger than I was prepared to receive that I still have no words to translate it. This answer felt deep and rich, like a humus-filled soil, but it did not feel personal. It seemed to me to be an answer that encompassed more than just myself, laden with possibilities of wholeness and creativity available to all who walk in human form.

We are so much more than we have allowed ourselves to be.

Who does our planet, Gaia, know us to be?

What relationships does she know us to be capable of?

What collaborative creations is she waiting to evolve with our heartfelt assistance?

We can only learn the answers to these questions through doing the work of connecting to our hearts, opening to their full abilities and using them to lead our head-brains on a path that will far exceed the hopes of sustainability. There is a world of natural collaborations, fractal infinities, and synergistic relationships to explore on this very living planet. The first step is inside you. Use your curious awareness to collaborate with your heart. You have the tools to do so now. Please use them.

Playtime! Celebrate

Congratulations for having read through this book! One of the most important things I have learned on my journey is that because we are always evolving, always learning, we will never be "perfect" and never be "done." It is, therefore, necessary to celebrate all the little things that we accomplish in a day.

If you have completed even one of the playtime exercises in this book, pat yourself on the back, whoop it up with your friends, or do something fun and relaxing for your nervous system. Sing, dance, move!

Celebrate yourself daily in some small way that nourishes all of you. That might mean taking a walk, enjoying a bubble bath, making some time to watch a sunset or moonrise, giving yourself some creative time to paint or write or play music. Taking this kind of time for yourself is an important part of establishing a natural collaboration with your heart. It is an important part of becoming a playfully and curiously aware human being; one living in collaboration with both life and Earth.

Remember that if you would like extra assistance in moving through any of the playtime exercises, audio versions of each of them are available through my website. Please visit: https://naturalcollaboration.com

Take a deep breath.
Relax.
I wish you great growing as you live in curious awareness, here, on Earth and within Gaia.

Acknowledgements

Writing a book is much like growing a garden: to do it well requires a great deal of collaboration. I am grateful to the many people, animals, and plants who have helped me with the process of imagining and then writing this book.

Many seeds were planted with my first group of inspired apprentices, whose authenticity and openness helped me to define and refine what I had to teach. Thank you Adam, Alana, Daniella, Emily, Eva, Kelly, Justin, Rob, and Suean. Special thanks go to Suean Stewart for many conversations over the past year, pushing and expanding both our edges.

Thanks to Dale and Diane Jacobson for giving me a place for much gardening and much learning. The Bluebird Farm-Garden has grown me as much as I have grown it.

I thank those who read some or all of the early manuscript giving me much needed feedback: Alana Lucia, George Nolte, Rob Stefke, and Logan Edwards. Much appreciation to Heather Borkowski, an insightful editing angel and also one of my early readers. I am so grateful that the Universe sent her to me. Christine Shugrue did a masterful job with proofreading. (And I made some more changes after she had it, so all errors are mine.) Thanks also to Jeff Kane whose comments on the first part of a late draft pushed me to make this book at least a little more readable.

I am also grateful for the generosity of Randy Griffis in creating the beautiful cover illustration that captures perfectly the essence of this book. And thanks to Autumn Barr for stepping in with technical help when I most needed it.

My husband, Tom Wade, has been a huge support in getting this book made; bouncing ideas around, making dinner when I was busy writing, and sharing his own passions for soil and life. I continue to be amazed and inspired by his dedication to wonder and to growth.

Then there are Zorro, Rose, and Topaz - who make every day better.

And finally, all those who will never read the words on this page, but who read them from my heart. You are the dearest and best of friends, and I am grateful for your love, support, and generosity: Viola, Hawthorne, Spilanthes, Rosa, Raspberry, Lamb's ear, Ragweed, Rosemary, Salvia, Lemon Verbena, silvery Artemesias, Solstice broccoli, Lettuce, Carrot, Strawberry, Tolli's sweet Italian pepper, Shisito pepper, Dester tomato, Oak, Pine, Fir, Cedar, Sequoia, Willow, Apple, Peach, Yew and many others. I am so glad to be here with all of you.

Sources and Resources

CHAPTER 1: AWARENESS IS YOUR MAGIC KEY

BODY AWARENESS
Hanna, Thomas. *Somatics: Reawakening the Mind's Control of Movement, Flexibility, and Health.* Cambridge: De Capo Press, 1988.

Mayfield, John, DC. *Body Intelligence: How to "Think" Outside Your Brain and Connect to Your Multi-Dimensional Self.* Grass Valley, CA: NuBalance Publishing, 2009.

Feldenkrais website: http://www.feldenkrais.com

QUANTUM PHYSICS
Double Slit Experiment explanation with graphics:
http://www.mysearch.org.uk/website1/html/546.Double-Slit.html

Goswami, Amit. *The Self-Aware Universe: How Consciousness Creates the Material World.* New York: Jeremy P Tarcher/Putnam, 1993.

McTaggart, Lynne. *The Bond: Connecting Through the Space Between Us.* New York: Free Press, 2011.

MORPHIC FIELDS AND THE WORK OF RUPERT SHELDRAKE
Sheldrake, Rupert. *Morphic Resonance: The Nature of Formative Causation.* Rochester, VT: Park Street Press, 2009. (This is an updated and expanded edition of *A New Science of Life.*)

Sheldrake, Rupert *The Science Delusion* TED Talk at TEDx Whitechapel: https://www.youtube.com/watch?v=JKHUaNAxsTg

Sheldrake's website: http://www.sheldrake.org

CHAPTER 2: OUR STORY POWER IS CREATIVE

STORY POWER
Arthur, Mary Alice. *Take Back the Power of Y(our) Story!* TED Talk at TEDx Kiel University
https://www.youtube.com/watch?feature=share&v=ilMwoEdqMTs&app=desktop

Meade, Michael. *The World Behind The World: Living at the Ends of Time*. Seattle: Greenfire Press, 2008.

PLACEBOS
Dispenza, Joe. *You are the Placebo: Making Your Mind Matter*. Carlsbad, CA: Hay House, Inc., 2014.

Talbot, Margaret. "The Placebo Prescription," *The New York Times*, January 9, 2000

Walker, Joseph. "Fake Knee Surgery as Good as Real Procedure, Study Finds," *The Wall Street Journal*, December 25, 2013.

VACCINES
Miller Neil. *The Vaccine Safety Manual for Concerned Families and Health Practitioners – A Guide to Immunization Risks and Protection*. Santa Fe, NM. New Atlantean Press, 2008.

Habakus, Louise and Holland, Mary. *Vaccine Epidemic: How Corporate Greed, Biased Science, and Coercive Government Threaten our Human Rights, and our Children*. New York: Skyhorse Publishing, 2012.

BRAIN HEALTH
Hanson, Rick, PhD and Mendius, Richard, MD. *Buddha's Brain: The Practical Neuroscience of Happiness, Love, and Wisdom*. Oakland, CA: New Harbinger Publications, Inc., 2009.

ELECTRIC SUN AND UNIVERSE

Bodanis, David. *Electric Universe: The Shocking True Story of Electricity*. New York: Crown Publishers, 2005. (Note: This author does not discuss the Electric Universe Theory, however, this is one of the most accessible and entertaining explanations of electricity that I have found.)

The Thunderbolts Project/Electric Universe Theory website: https://www.thunderbolts.info/wp/

Scott, Donald E. *The Electric Sky*. Milwaukie, OR: Mikamar Publishing, 2012.

LIVING UNIVERSE

Sams, Gregory. *Sun of gOd: Discover the Self-Organizing Consciousness That Underlies Everything*. San Francisco: Weiser Books, 2009.

Sheldrake, Rupert. *Is the Sun Conscious?* audio program listed under "Full Seminars, Lectures and Dialogues. (36 min): http://www.sheldrake.org/audios

FRACTALS AND BOUNDED INFINITIES

Fractals: Hunting the Hidden Dimension, PBS Nova, 2008. https://www.youtube.com/watch?v=HvXbQb57lsE

Mandelbrot, Benoit. *The Fractal Geometry of Nature*. New York: W.H, Freeman & Company, 1982.

Haramein, Nassim. *Black Whole* (DVD). Boulder: Gaiam, 2011.

BREATHING

Melaine, Dolli. *How to Take a Healthy Breath*. Grass Valley, CA: Teahouse of Danger, 2012

CHAPTER 3: COLLABORATIVE INTELLIGENCE DRIVES EVOLUTION

COLLABORATIVE INTELLIGENCE:
Boone, J. Allen. *Kinship with All Life*. San Francisco: Harper San Francisco, 1954.

Capra, Fritjof. *The Web of Life: A New Scientific Understanding of Living Systems*. New York: Doubleday, 1996.

Mollison, Bill. *Permaculture: A Designer's Manual*. Tyalgum, Australia: Tagari Publications, 1988.

Montgomery, David R. and Bikle, Anne. *The Hidden Half of Nature: The Microbial Roots of Life and Health*. New York: W.W. Norton & Company: 2016.

Ohlson, Kristin. *The Soil Will Save Us: How Scientists, Farmers, and Foodies Are Healing the Soil to Save the Planet*. New York: Rodale, 2014.

Stamets, Paul. *Mycelium Running: How Mushrooms Can Help Save the World*. Berkeley, CA:Ten Speed Press, 2005.

What Plants Talk About, PBS Nature, 2014. (Documentary Video): https://www.youtube.com/watch?v=CrrSAc-vjG4)

EPIGENETICS:
Lipton, Bruce. *The Biology of Belief: Unleashing the Power of Consciousness, Matter, and Miracles*. Carlsbad, CA: Hay House, Inc., 2008.

MICROBIOLOGY OF THE HUMAN GUT:
Perlmutter, David, MD. *Brain Maker: The Power of Gut Microbes to Heal and Protect Your Brain - for Life* . New York: Little, Brown & Company, 2015.

Sonnenberg, Justin and Sonnenberg, Erica. *The Good Gut: Taking Control of Your Weight, Your Mood, and Your Long Term Health.* New York: Penguin Press, 2015.

CHAPTER 4: YOUR HEART IS NOT A PUMP

HEART INTELLIGENCE:
Buhner, Stephen Harrod. *The Secret Teachings of Plants: The Intelligence of the Heart in the Direct Perception of Nature.* Rochester, VT: Bear & Co, 2004.

Goldstein, Barry. *The Secret Language of the Heart: How to Use Music, Sound, and Vibration as Tools for Healing and Personal Transformation.* San Antonio, TX: Hierophant Publishing, 2016.

Keasbey, Heather Luna. "Hawthorn~Healer of the Heart" blog post for Nevada City Herb & Tea Co. website: http://www.ncherbandtea.com/blogs/news/45981761-hawthorn-healer-of-the-heart

HeartMath Institute. *Science of the Heart: Exploring the Role of the Heart in Human Performance.* Free PDF download from their website: https://www.heartmath.org/research/

Pearce, Joseph Chilton. *The Heart-Mind Matrix: How the Heart Can Teach the Mind New Ways to Think.* Rochester, VT: Park Street Press, 2012.

CHAPTER 5: NATURE IS A NERVOUS SYSTEM

PLANT INTELLIGENCE:
Buhner, Stephen Harrod. *Plant Intelligence and the Imaginal Realm: Beyond the Doors of Perception into the Dreaming of Earth.* Rochester, VT: Bear & Co, 2014.

"Memory in Plants" in *The Economist,* January 19, 2014: http://www.economist.com/blogs/babbage/2014/01/botany

Montgomery, Pam. *Plant Spirit Healing: A Guide to Working with Plant Consciousness.* Rochester, VT: Bear & Co, 2008.

What Plants Talk About, PBS Nature, 2014.(Documentary video): https://www.youtube.com/watch?v=CrrSAc-vjG4)

NATURE'S INTELLIGENCE:
Callahan, Philip S. *Tuning in to Nature: Infrared Radiation and the Insect Communication System.* Austin, TX: Acres U.S.A., 2001.

—— *Paramagnetism: Rediscovering Nature's Secret Force of Growth.* Austin, TX: Acres U.S.A., 1995.

Citro, Massimo, MD, *The Basic Code of the Universe: The Science of the Invisible in Physics, Medicine, and Spirituality.* Rochester, VT: Park Street Press, 2011.

Narby, Jeremy. *Intelligence in Nature: An Inquiry into Knowledge.* New York: Jeremy P Tarcher/Penguin, 2005.

CHAPTER 6: LIFE IS ONE WHOLE

Bach, Richard. *One.* New York: Dell Publishing, 1989.

McTaggart, Lynne. *The Bond: Connecting Through the Space Between Us.* New York: Free Press, 2011.

Montgomery, David R. and Bikle, Anne. *The Hidden Half of Nature: The Microbial Roots of Life and Health.* New York: W.W. Norton & Company: 2016.

Talbot, Michael. *The Holographic Universe.* New York: HarperCollins, 1991.

What Plants Talk About, PBS Nature, 2014. (Documentary Video): https://www.youtube.com/watch?v=CrrSAc-vjG4)

CHAPTER 7: FOOD CIRCULATES LOVE AND CONNECTION

SOILS:

Brunetti, Jerry. *The Farm as Ecosystem: Tapping Nature's Reservoir - Biology, Geology, Diversity*. Austin, TX: Acres U.S.A, 2014.

Montgomery, David R. and Bikle, Anne. *The Hidden Half of Nature: The Microbial Roots of Life and Health*. New York: W.W. Norton & Company: 2016.

Soil Food Web, Inc. Dr. Elaine Ingham is the mother of our current understanding of soil biology. Her website is: http://www.soilfoodweb.com

Tompkins, Peter. *Secrets of the Soil: New Age Solutions for Restoring Our Planet*. New York: Harper & Row, 1990.

AGRICULTURE AND HEALTH:
Frisch, Tracy. "The Future of Better Pest Management: Interview with Jonathan Lundgren." *Acres USA*. February, 2016.

Miller, Daphne. *Farmacology: What Innovative Family Farming Can Teach Us About Health and Healing*. New York: HarperCollins Publishers, 2013.

Montgomery, David R. and Bikle, Anne. *The Hidden Half of Nature: The Microbial Roots of Life and Health*. New York: W.W. Norton & Company: 2016.

CHAPTER 8: YOU ARE AN INTELLIGENT CELL IN THE GAIAN
BODY

EARTH HISTORY:
Capra, Fritjof. *The Web of Life: A New Scientific Understanding of Living Systems*. New York: Doubleday, 1996.

PLANT AND ANIMAL COMMUNICATION:
*The Animal Communicator*Anna Breytenbach**, Foster Brothers Film Productions for NHU Africa, 2015:
https://www.youtube.com/watch?v=iEALi7ZEbCo

Buhner, Stephen Harrod. *The Secret Teachings of Plants: The Intelligence of the Heart in the Direct Perception of Nature.* Rochester, VT: Bear & Co, 2004.

Findhorn Community. *The Findhorn Garden: Pioneering a New Vision of Man and Nature in Cooperation*. New York: HarperCollins, 1976.

Maclean, Dorothy. *To Hear The Angels Sing*. Traverse City, MI: Lorian Press, 2008.

Roads, Michael J. *Talking with Nature: Sharing the Energies and Spirit of Trees, Plants, Birds, and Earth.* Tiburon, CA: H J Kramer, Inc., 1987.

----- *Journey Into Nature: A Spiritual Adventure*. Tiburon, CA: H J Kramer, Inc., 1990.

----- *Journey Into Oneness: A Spiritual Odyssey*. Tiburon, CA: H J Kramer, Inc., 1994.

----- *Into a Timeless Realm: A Metaphysical Adventure*. Tiburon, CA: H J Kramer, Inc., 1995.

Wright, Machaelle Small. *Behaving as if the God in All Life Mattered*. Warrenton, VA: Perelandra Ltd., 1997.

----- *Perelandra Garden Workbook: A Complete Guide to Gardening with Nature Intelligences.* Warrenton, VA: Perelandra, 1993.

A TASTE OF NEW PARADIGM SOLUTIONS
Most of the books and videos listed above fall in this category. In addition, here are a few more suggestions for further exploration.

Capra, Fritjof and Mattei, Ugo. *The Ecology of Law: Toward a Legal System in Tune with Nature and Community.* Perret-Koehler Publishers, 2015.

Franckh, Pierre. *The DNA Field and the Law of Resonance: Creating Reality Through Conscious Thought.* Rochester, VT: Destiny Books, 2014.

Gregory, Danny. *Art Before Breakfast: A Zillion Ways to be More Creative No Matter How Busy You Are.* San Francisco: Chronicle Books, 2015.

Holzer, Sepp. *Desert or Paradise: Restoring Endangered Landscapes Using Water Management, including Lake and Pond Construction.* White River Junction, VT: Chelsea Green Publishing, 2011.

McKusick, Eileen Day. *Tuning the Human Biofield: Healing with Vibrational Sound Therapy.* Rochester, VT: Healing Arts Press, 2014. (This is an awesome book! It contains a wonderful, clear description of the Electric Universe Theory in chapter 4.)

Phillips, Michael. *The Holistic Orchard: Tree Fruits and Berries the Biological Way.* White River Junction, VT: Chelsea Green Publishing, 2011.

Tessler, Bari. *The Art of Money: A Life-Changing Guide to Financial Happiness.* Berkeley, CA: Parallax Press, 2016. (This book offers an excellent framework for using curious awareness to heal and change your relationship with money from the inside out.)

Thomson, Gesine. *Exploring the Mind* TED Talk: TEDx Kish
http://tedxtalks.ted.com/video/Exploring-the-mind-Gesine-Thoms

3D Ocean Farming: http://greenwave.org/3d-ocean-farming/ (Bren Smith and team are modeling collaborative intelligence by growing food with the rhythm of the ocean, while also cleaning up pollution from land-based agriculture, building resilience to climate change, and creating economic opportunity for others.)

ABOUT THE AUTHOR

RENEE WADE is a certified Permaculture designer, an award-winning gardener, and a plant communicator with over 25 years of experience in ecological design. She specializes in creating lush, holistic gardens that grow food, beauty, and connection. She makes her home in the foothills of the Sierra Nevada mountains.

Her website is www.NaturalCollaboration.com.

www.ingramcontent.com/pod-product-compliance
Lightning Source LLC
Chambersburg PA
CBHW030018290326
41934CB00005B/393